Work and the Human Spirit

Work
and the
Human
Spirit

◆◆◆◆◆◆

By John Scherer
with
Larry Shook

JS&A

Published by John Scherer & Associates
The Paulsen Center
421 W. Riverside Suite 1000
Spokane, WA 99201
800/727-9115 509/838-8167
Fax: 509/623-2511

Library of Congress Catalog Card Number: 93-92789

ISBN 0-9639348-0-5 (paperback)

Cover design by Klundt & Hosmer Design Associates Inc.

Text Illustrations by Rick Hosmer

Printed in the United States of America

Second Printing

DEDICATION

For Boone, Jack, J.J., and the others

TABLE OF CONTENTS

Work and the Human Spirit

Introduction

THIS BOOK IS A COLLECTION OF LITTLE STORIES, small dramas that revolve around a common theme. Exactly what to label the theme I don't know. Call it "the human heart at work," or "work and the human spirit." If a better label occurs to you after you read the stories, by all means use it. The stories, by the way, are all true, and all of them are told with permission. Of course, the names of the players have been changed—even brave people deserve their privacy.

The stage upon which our mini-dramas unfold is an unusual personal development program called the "Executive Development Intensive." Senior executives and their spouses attend it for the purpose of gaining insights about themselves, insights which their companies believe will improve their effectiveness as guides in the wilderness of our strange times.

The Executive Development Intensive (EDI, as its alumni call it) is unique in the ranks of management development programs for several reasons. First, because it wasn't born of abstract theory, or of a marketing scheme to push a package of techniques. Instead it was "pulled" into existence by the chief executive officer of a multinational European company. He wanted a program where his managers could truly find themselves and therefore find greater effectiveness. Second, it addresses the whole person—body, mind and spirit—in an integrated way. And finally, it is a solo experience, not a group experience. Only the executive and spouse are present with the staff, ensuring privacy in addressing deep questions of individual purpose.

The intensely personal work that takes place is both mundane and (in my view anyway) profound. Also, you should know that it reflects a hunch now shared by a small but growing number of the Western world's business thinkers.

The hunch is this: the quality of work we do cannot be separated from the quality of "self" we manage to create in our lives. If the hunch is accurate, it has at least two important implications for every company.

1. Organizations have a vested interest in nurturing the human spirit of the workforce, since the state of workers' spirits has a direct bearing upon the quality of their work. And because leaders act as "speed governors" on the rest of the organization, it will help businesses to have people at the top who are awakening their own spirits.

2. Work that injures the human spirit, even if it's profitable, isn't good work in the end; companies ought to change that work as quickly as possible, because the forces of the marketplace (or the forces of the universe or whatever you want to call them) tend eventually to punish soul-killing labor out of existence anyway.

In a sense, these notions aren't the least bit controversial. Most companies, after all, care about the morale of their workers and do what they can to keep it up. But at another level the ideas are radical. Ever since Descartes persuaded the world that the body and mind are separate, most work has been organized around the assumption that, as many managers have told me, "The human spirit—whatever that is—doesn't have a damn to do with making money. And even if it does, a worker's spirit is nobody's business but the worker's." And so to the extent that companies start caring about the quality of the inner lives of those who serve their customers, and start acting on that concern, they will inevitably transform the world at work.

Up until now the conventional wisdom has been that economic prosperity has tradeoffs. We have been expected to choose between career and family. Between jobs and the environment. Between happiness, achievement, security, and sanity. The stories in this book make it clear just how heavy the personal costs of this thinking have been. These executives are highly successful and very creative men and women, which is why their companies sent them. They are "winners," but their losses have been great; far greater than they or anyone else would choose for himself or herself, greater in fact than most people would wish on their worst enemies.

During our work over the last several years we have taken the casualty reports...

Of the young fast tracker who used his Harvard MBA to land the dream job, only to learn that "after four or five months, I absolutely hated it." Nevertheless, he stayed with the dream until we met him in his mid-thirties, a man with everything he had hoped for but nothing he wanted.

Of the brilliant woman in her late fifties whose role in the down-sizing of her huge company jolted her into the realization that in her rise to the top she had jettisoned the warmth, the spontaneity, the ability to play, which had been the core of her personality, and the source of her joy and satisfaction.

Of the fair-haired boy who ultimately bolted rather than endure the "slow suffocation" of life in the executive suite of his Fortune 500 company. "The closer I got to the kinds of decisions that the very top of the organization was making, the more senseless I found them," he told us. "The corruption of the human spirit at work was occurring more at the top than anywhere else, and affecting everyone in the organization."

Of the executive's wife who after twenty-nine years of marriage suddenly found herself hospitalized for acute depression when her husband was transferred for the twelfth time. She told us of the deep love she and her mate shared, of his valiant efforts to be provider, husband, and father, only to have his daughter at one point giving up on ever having an intimate relationship with him, and his son think of him as "the man in the living room behind the newspaper."

Why would companies sponsor such soul-searching on the part of their senior executives if it leads to such grim conclusions? Because grim conclusions aren't the only outcome of frankly inventorying one's condition. Cancer undiagnosed is still cancer. Cancer discovered early can often be cured. In their intensive work, each of those cited above identified the personal decisions—often unconscious—that had led to their dark night of the soul, and it helped them glimpse new possibilities that had long been invisible to them. In those new possibilities lie new frontiers for the work of their lives. And it is along those frontiers, the frontiers of the human spirit, that the new world of work awaits discovery.

I happen to believe that we have reached a fortuitous fork in the road, where what it takes for *companies* to survive is also what it takes for the *individuals* who make them up to survive. The highest goals of any business can best be realized by awakening and nurturing the human spirit of the people who comprise it—its leaders, its employees and even its customers.

We are now at a point where the speed of change and the kinds of issues that are confronting organizations—economic, social, political, environmental—are proving to be insurmountable. We have companies like IBM, General Motors, Sears, beehives of resourcefulness whose performance for generations was more than equal to the onslaughts of competitors and market fluctuations. Today, these giants find themselves as vulnerable as the most fragile new business start-up. The twentieth century is not yet over and already we find ourselves haunted by the ghosts of corporate giants who wrote important chapters of this eventful period of history. What the deceased companies lacked, and what those struggling to reinvent themselves need, is a quality of performance that can't be produced by doing more-of-the-same-only-better.

On this there is much learned opinion. Management guru Peter Drucker, for instance, chides America's largest companies for changing everything about themselves but the one thing they must change—their concept of business. MIT's Peter Senge, in his book *The Fifth Discipline: The Art of the Learning Organization* argued eloquently for a new way of doing business in which workers are deeply, not superficially, engaged in their work.

Work and the Human Spirit is based on this belief: the huge challenges facing the workplace today are not going to be overcome with new management theories or motivational tips and techniques. Even such radical organizational surgery as reengineering has shown itself to not be enough. I happen to believe that we are in a crisis which must be approached as something so profound, so fundamental, so universal, that it can only be resolved at the level of the human spirit.

If you are willing to consider the possibility of doing business from the perspective of the human spirit, then also consider one other possibility. From now on the bottom line in your business, just like your health as an individual, is not the goal but the score card. Not your purpose, but an unforgiving feedback mechanism. As one who has had the privilege of working with some of the best companies and most inquiring executives in the country, it is clear to me that something is off, *way off*, in the way we have come to understand the problems of the workplace and the solutions we hope will work. We have fundamental relearning to do as we try to get at the heart of things. A few brave souls are leading the way, and this book is a sampling of their stories.

Executives who don't explore for new concepts of themselves can scarcely be expected to explore for, and discover, new concepts for their business. And can workers who decline to engage deeply with the miracle of their own lives be expected to engage deeply with their work? Susan Gretchko, a colleague, puts it this way: "We tend to think that we have two lives, a work life and a personal life. I remind clients that you only have one life, and it's all very personal.

Find a larger purpose, engage deeply with your work, and relate to people. These are becoming the new prescriptions for how to succeed in business. In the end I think we will learn that they are remedies not to be found in the study of business but rather in what should be a prerequisite course—the study of who we are as human beings. Ours is a time of great need and great challenge. Some people say that the dominant reality of current history is that we have met the limitations of our outer world, and that the ramifications are clear: the air we breathe is at risk, the water we drink is at risk, and our cities are too crowded. I suspect that it is really our *inner* world that is choking us, and that what is happening outside is merely a symptom.

As it always does, the marketplace is giving us valuable feedback if we can just learn to interpret it correctly. Almost with a single voice consumers are saying that if you want their business, you've got to give them something of value. Real value—we have begun the painful process of learning—can only be given by people who know their own value.

Question: How can any of us ever know our true value if we never take inventory?

The stories in this book are of people taking inventory of themselves. I think of them as the first restless explorers who are impatient with the limitations of the old world, men and women who sense something bright and wonderful just over the horizon, a new purpose worth taking risks for. What do they risk? Nothing less than their very way of *being* in the world. What do they gain for their troubles? A sense of wealth, as one of the program's early faculty members, Dixon de Leña, put it. Wealth that was in their possession at birth and cannot be taken away, wealth that is not of this world.

Every company and every person trying to make it in the world must learn about this asset. How can they learn? One way is to listen to the explorers, like those whose plain and simple stories are recorded here.

1
The Phone
Call

CALL THE MAN CARL. I'll probably never really understand what led him to phone me, but what he said, in a delightful Dutch accent beamed into my Spokane, Washington office by an orbiting satellite, was something like this:

"John! I've got a man here who I think has the capacity to be a Director, but I'm a little uncertain about whether he is right for the job. Would you meet with him for two or three days and then tell me whether you think he's the man I'm looking for?"

A year earlier I had met Carl at a conference in Cambridge, England. He was the CEO of a multi-national company, one of the largest employers in his country. He was joined at the conference by the top executives from his headquarters, plus the general manager and chief financial officer from each of the twelve countries in which Carl's company operated subsidiaries. At the conference, I had given a presentation on breakthrough thinking and apparently something I said sparked Carl's call.

The trouble was, he was asking me to provide a service, which I did not provide and don't imagine I ever will. The simple

reason is that I consider people to be works in progress. I am interested, in fact, fascinated, by the nature of that work and its various
stages. But in a world where rivers wander, continents drift,
nations come and go, and people never cease to be amazing in
their ability to adjust to their changing world, I'm much more
intrigued by what each of us might become than what we happen
to be at any given time. I am haunted by a notion that lingers from
my days as a Lutheran minister, something about God not yet
being done with us.

I thanked Carl but declined his request. Instead, I made a
counteroffer off the top of my head. I suggested to Carl that I
spend the two or three days with his executive by helping him
conduct a kind of intense inquiry of himself. At the end of the
executive's exploration, the two of us would prepare a joint report
on what we considered to be his strengths and his developmental
areas. The two of us, I proposed, would tell Carl if we felt the
director-to-be was ready, and if so, under what conditions.

In the quiet that followed, you might have heard the faint
whistling of wind in the stars. Finally, the silence was broken.
"Okay," Carl said. He couldn't have known how hard I
swallowed. I had never done anything like this before, but if my
caller sensed that, he never let on. Carl said he would brief his
executive and ask him to get in touch with me to coordinate
further. I sat back in my chair and wondered what in the world I

had gotten myself into.

Two hours later my phone rang again. This time it was the candidate himself. Call him Hans. Although it must have been midnight on his side of the world, his tone was lively. As soon as he spoke, I remembered him from the conference, a classic "people person," a warm, personable man, instantly likeable. I asked him how he felt about the arrangement. "I'm a little scared," I remember him telling me. "I have a funny feeling this is going to be a different experience for me, not what I'm used to."

You're scared? I thought. In my calmest, most professional voice I asked him what he would like to come out of his trip to Spokane. "I don't know," he said. "Just *do me.* I want to develop myself in every possible direction." I asked if he would be open to a body/mind/spirit approach. He indicated he would.

Carl, the boss of the director-to-be, is an exceptional individual. He is brilliant, compassionate, and one of the most strikingly candid people I have ever met. His company is the kind of prosperous, humanistic organization where anyone would want to work. And serving as a director of Carl's company is precisely the sort of career pinnacle most executives dream of. Directors of Carl's company are given a piece of the rock, and they are expected to nurture its future not merely through the exercises of their imagination but through brave truth telling. (The colorful tribal rites of the human organization don't always celebrate honesty. In my work with organizations I have experienced a thousand times the strangely elaborate, always unspoken, self-defeating reward system that Mark Twain liked to call "deflecting from the perpendicular.") So a heavy sense of responsibility weighed down on me, responsibility to Carl, to his company, to this man who was traveling to the other side of the world for no other reason—it is possible that Hans didn't realize this at the time—than to have a conversation with himself. Last but not least, I felt a responsibility to myself. I took this request as an invitation to enter a new and unknown territory.

Long before my guest ever boarded his airplane for Spokane I had created a plan. I could only hope that Hans had a touch of the explorer in him, for what I had in mind would expand his mind, stretch his body, and deepen his spirit. If the experience was a success, he would return home with a clearer picture not just of who he already was, but with a new understanding of what else he might be, both as an executive and as a human being. It is my bias that treasure lies in tiny discoveries like these. Figuring out how to express this wealth on a balance sheet is a challenge, however, and in general I respect the corporate decorum that respects the private lives of workers. But you don't have to be religious to suspect that there is more to life than meets the eye.

The mind and its conclusions may be a highly defended fortress, but it can be breached. One way you can sneak into it is through the back door which is the body itself. We are learning that our experience of the world, our knowledge, is stored not just in the brain but throughout the tissues of the body. Certain kinds of bodywork can liberate us from misconceptions, can relax the mind into discovering broader realities, and can help us see the world in new ways.

And so when my guest arrived in Spokane an unusual little team was waiting for him. It was a highly focused task force that would fuel him with nutrition, exercise with him, massage him, and escort him on his journey of self-reflection.

In the end, the director-to-be had an encounter with himself that led to profound insights. Hans learned that his great strength of creating agreement among colleagues was laced with a fear of disappointing people, or making them unhappy, and that this fear was no ally of a corporate director. He even remembered the childhood events that had caused the fear—"remembered" isn't exactly the right word, because he was unaware of ever having given them a moment's thought. Hans learned something about the sense of humor that was a hallmark of his personality. It had an edge to it. And the edge came from a subtle feeling of anger. The anger came from his belief that people took advantage of him. No sooner did that occur to him than he realized how he was actually in cahoots with his exploiters. Because he was so reluctant to disappoint people or make them unhappy, he let them push him around. This made him resentful. Because he was such a nice guy, he didn't want to say anything. So he mined his humor with little barbs. Of course this appalled him, because it wasn't at all in keeping with his deep kindness and affection toward people.

It wasn't much more than a week after Hans had returned home than the satellite brought Carl's voice to me again. "What did you do to Hans?" he asked.

My heart started pounding. When Hans left, I truly did not know what, if any, meaningful benefit he might have retained from his experience. I knew that some insights came to him, and I knew that we had shared a few powerful moments. But I had no way of telling what "stuck." There was a paradox in my mind, which was this: you don't nurture your human spirit for the bucks; you do it for your spirit. The bucks either come or they don't. (But, my advice to pension fund managers: don't put your money in companies that ignore the human spirit.)

"What is it, Carl?" I asked.

"Well, in our board meetings, he speaks his mind. Not all the time, I still have to ask him occasionally, but he's taking risks I haven't seen before. He acts serious when he needs to be, seems more of a straight shooter. John I think we've got a new man here."

If Carl thought he detected the whistling of wind in the

stars, it was just me exhaling. "Well, great," I said. "Glad to hear it."

He said, "Listen, John, I would like to send..." and he began naming other executives he wanted to book on flights to Spokane. That conversation turned out to be the beginning of what became the Executive Development Intensive, the EDI.

In the next year, six other senior executives from Carl's company followed Hans to Spokane. We greeted them at Spokane International like relatives from the old country. During their time with us they ate well, exercised, breathed, had their muscles kneaded, spent time alone, and talked for hours and hours—to us, to themselves—until they learned new things about their lives. They enjoyed a celebration dinner with us on their last evening and we talked the whole thing over. Then they flew away, and we stayed in touch—with letters, phone calls, little gifts—like fellow members of a far-flung explorers club. In the seven years that have passed since Carl's phone call, the trickle of European executives has been followed by a steady stream of other executives and their spouses, over two hundred now, from twelve nations.

About a year after Carl first contacted me, I asked why he wanted his executives to have the experience they did. He told me that it was intuition. He explained that there were plenty of industrial psychologists and therapists in his country, but that it wasn't therapy, at least not in the conventional sense, that he felt was missing from his managers' lives. Also, he said, there was no shortage of management assessment centers, but that they only evaluate how well people "manage their *in* box." He told me he was looking for something deeper.

I thought I knew what he meant. I'd had a life-changing experience or two of my own. One took place in the middle of the Atlantic Ocean.

2

The Phantom

WHEN I WAS A YOUNG MAN I had a terrifying experience of self-discovery. I wouldn't wish the trauma on anyone. But the gift of the discovery by itself, were it mine to give, I would give to everyone.

By the winter of 1963, following graduation from Roanoke College, I landed in the U.S. Navy as an officer aboard a destroyer, USS EATON (DD-510). The work had a depressing beginning.

Just two days before setting out on my first Mediterranean cruise I found myself standing at rigid attention on EATON'S deck with my shipmates. Tears were streaming down our cheeks as a 21-gun salute boomed over the harbor of Norfolk, Virginia. President Kennedy had been assassinated. With the nation grieving its fallen president, we put to sea on November 25, part of a carrier group steaming toward the Strait of Gibraltar.

A day out of Cape Hatteras a hurricane started to follow us. We turned right to let the bad weather pass. The hurricane turned with us. By degrees we kept turning right, but like a predator stalking, the wind tracked us, then pounced. For three days it mauled us. We took the sea on the port bow, green water crashing over the bridge, which should have been thirty-eight feet above the ocean. It was like an endless roller coaster ride. One sickening roll was recorded on the EATON'S inclinometer at 44°. We were saved from capsizing by the capricious harmonics of the sea that sent an odd wave to buoy us at just the right moment. At one point I was nearly swept overboard. For three days I vomited, until the yellow bile of my stomach lining started coming up. Between watches a kindly steward named Jones escorted me to my bunk, tucked me in, and spoon-fed me broth and crackers to prevent dehydration. The hurricane released us on November 30. We licked our wounds for a day and made repairs. The following day was when the Phantom jet went in.

I had intended to offer the Navy my services as the pilot of just such an airplane. But when my left eye went 20/40 my senior year in college, my dreams of being a naval aviator ended. At Officers Candidate School someone suggested I could still fly by becoming a Radar Intercept Officer (RIO), the man who rides behind the pilot. It seemed like a great idea until I learned that the RIO handles all the radio communication. There was one small problem with this idea: I was a stutterer. From the time I was ten years old, I lived in terror of beginning sentences for fear that they would be hiding words I couldn't say, words beginning with the hard sounds like "t" or "b" or "k" or "g". Some people live with chronic pain or low-grade headaches. I lived with a low-grade fear of stuttering. So, in 1963, I decided to take my chances on a destroyer where, I hoped, I wouldn't have to talk much.

In its infinite wisdom, the Navy, of course, made me an air controller. That is how Ensign Scherer, just weeks out of training, green at the gills after the hurricane, came to be standing watch in the middle of the night when a voice as deep as God's came over the radio.

"Hermit," said the voice, "this is Climax Himself, over."

I broke out in a cold sweat. "Hermit" was my ship's call sign. "Climax" was the call sign of one of the most formidable ships ever to sail, the aircraft carrier USS ENTERPRISE, one of the heavies we were escorting across the Atlantic. "Climax Himself" was ENTERPRISE'S Captain.

"We just lost a Foxtrot Four out your way," he said. "I hereby designate you Sierra Alpha Romeo Charlie. Keep me posted on this net. Find 'em, Hermit! Over!"

Translation: An F-4 Phantom jet had crashed. I was deputized on the spot as Search And Rescue Coordinator, because, through an uncanny convergence of circumstances, I had the watch in the Combat Information Center on the ship nearest the crash.

At this point in my life it would have been hard to find a more difficult word for me to pronounce than "Climax." When I found out we were going to be Plane-Guard for the Big E and that her call sign was Climax, just thinking about calling her on the radio caused an invisible fist to close on my throat. I had to use every trick known to stutterers, like saying an easy word— "Roger" was my standby—to get the air moving over the vocal chords. So here was an unlucky situation for all concerned—not least of which were the two men down in the water. Fresh out of Air Control School, except for easy training exercises, I had never controlled a real, live airplane.

Nevertheless, I took a grease pencil, donned headphones, and sat down before the radar screen, which had become a snowstorm of blips. Pushing the "pickle" on my radio headset, sending my voice out over a thousand square miles of air and ocean, I said, "Any aircraft from Climax, this is Hermit. Check this net, over."

Out of the inky night the voices started coming back. "Ah, Roger, Hermit, this is Climax two-three, I have two-four and two-five in tow, request vector, over."

And a confident voice I'd never heard before said something like, "Roger, two-three, make a standard right turn for ID," and then, "I've got you, two-three, vector one-eight-five, descend to two thousand feet. Last known position about your one o'clock, five miles." The dialogues started just like that and it went on for over twenty-four hours.

When we graduated from Air Control School, they told us we most likely would never have to control more than four or five aircraft at a time. Now I had fifteen to twenty planes on my screen, converging at top speed toward my ship. I had to know that the two-zero sequence aircraft were Phantoms, that the three and four-zeros were Corsairs, the five-zeros were A-4s, and the seven-zeros were S2Fs, prop jobs. They moved at different speeds, had different fuel requirements, and I had to stack them accordingly and keep them from colliding. I had to fashion them into a giant mobile with a thousand feet of vertical separation, and I had to manipulate the mobile over the ocean in squares that expanded outward from the "datum," the last known position of the lost Phantom. And I had to keep talking.

Three or four hours into the ordeal, during a lull in the action, it dawned on me that not only had I not stuttered, I hadn't even *thought* about it. Never in my life had it occurred to me that John Jacob Scherer IV was anything other than a hopeless stutterer. I'll never forget the feelings of amazement, exhilaration, and gratitude that swept over me at that moment. The night wore on, turned into day, and then into night again. As the only controller on our little ship qualified to control jets, I had to stay on the scope the whole time, living on coffee and sandwiches, my concentration punctuated only by rare, frantic trips to the bathroom.

In the end, at about sunup the next day, we found the pilot but couldn't find his Radar Intercept Officer. It was very sad.

Climax himself sent a helicopter from ENTERPRISE to bring his flyer home.

As the pilot was being hoisted from the water he had the rescue diver contact our bridge. "Hermit, where's your air controller?" The captain called me to the bridge. "Guy out there wants to see you," he said.

The pilot and I were looking at each other over the water. I gave him a thumbs-up. Dangling from the hoist, just before he disappeared into the helicopter, the pilot, a lieutenant commander, saluted me. I had helped find his Phantom. He didn't know it, but he had also helped me find mine.

3

The Parsonage and

the Ashram

THEORETICALLY I KNEW that such personal transformation was possible. I had seen it repeatedly while growing up. I had just never experienced it in my own life. I had in fact been steeped in the opposite, reared between poles of transcendence and chaos, between my own family, a family whose patriarch served an entire community's faith.

I literally grew up in the parsonage of the First English Lutheran Church at Lombardy and Monument, Richmond, Virginia. My grandfather was pastor there for fifty years and I grew up there because my grandparents and the parsonage entourage raised me. My father was a brilliant man who entered college when he was fifteen. An alcoholic and sometime newspaperman, Pop did not work very much. My mother, who graduated *cum laude* from Bryn Mawr, worked hard at editorial jobs to support us. As a result, in one way or another, neither of them was home much.

It is tempting for me to say that Granddaddy raised me, but that would not be quite accurate. Granddaddy was my rock. In a world of chaos, he was a fixed reference by which I could navigate. From my vantage point every Sunday morning, he always looked more like a mountain than a man behind the pulpit, one of God's landmarks. Just to be with him, to climb up into his lap while he scribbled his sermon, to sit quietly beside him in a duck blind or fishing boat, made everything all right.

Orbiting about the mountain of my grandfather at the parsonage were two angels who attended to him and nurtured me. One of the angels was Sister Ruth, a Lutheran Deaconess, five feet tall and five feet wide. From Sister Ruth I learned what unconditional love and selfless service are. More than once when I needed shoes, it was Sister Ruth who took me shopping, purchasing them herself on her meager $10 weekly income. I'll take to my grave the life-sustaining memory—body and soul—of what it was to snuggle as a little boy into the pillowy bosom of Sister Ruth.

The other angel was Anabelle, the cook. Anabelle taught herself to read from comic books and these were the texts she used in teaching me to read. In the early 1940s, long before I was a sailor, Anabelle drafted me into the light infantry of her kitchen. She armed me with a spatula, taught me to shoulder it like a color guardsman, and then called musical cadence for me as I marched back and forth in the kitchen, a toy soldier on parade.

From the time I was five years old, I saw a steady stream of callers—from Governors to gardeners—come to see my grandfather. They arrived like fugitives escaping some unknown troubles. But then, a short while later, they would stroll out the door with the song of God in their hearts. I remember thinking as I got older, "What's going on in there?"

Granddaddy rarely talked about himself, but the Reverend John Jacob Scherer, Jr. is still something of a legend around Richmond. It wasn't until I grew up that I learned that not all parish pastors sit as judges on the benches of juvenile and domestic relations courts, and are founders of mental health associations, and schools of social work. President Roosevelt appointed him to the National Labor Relations Board. He was chaplain of the state prison and advisor to countless government and business leaders.

As a boy, I heard countless stories that celebrated his sixth sense about people and his unorthodox ways of reaching them. Typical of these legends was the account of three young boys who were brought before Judge Scherer's bench for breaking into a jewelry store and stealing watches. Two of the boys admitted their guilt and were sentenced accordingly. The third boy, for his intransigent silence, was sentenced to "go fishing with the judge three Saturdays in a row." Oral history has it that the first two Saturday's came and went, during which time the thief had nothing to say. On the third Saturday, the man and the boy baited their hooks, fished for hours, and ate their sandwiches. Not a word was spoken. "Well, I guess I blew this one," Granddaddy thought. The fishermen tied up, unloaded the boat and headed for the car.

At that moment, as though it were an intersection in time created just for the boy's transformation, he turned to my grandfather and said, "Judge, I took those watches." They stood there on the dock and had a long conversation. In that moment something in the boy's heart was healed. He grew up to become a Richmond bank president.

Of course, no one's life is an unbroken string of victories, and like everyone else, my grandfather suffered personal and professional losses. No loss in my grandfather's life, however, could compare with the loss of his only son, my father, John Jacob Scherer III, to alcoholism. There are those who could look at Pop's life and say he never had a chance, the scion of a great man who had time to minister to the wide world, but not to his own family. In the easy clinical jargon of our times, my father's family would be readily diagnosed as "dysfunctional." Granddaddy was never home, and Pop was surrounded by women—a gracious but doting mother, three sisters, and a bevy of various aunts and maids.

When Pop's precociousness thrust him into college at the tender age of fifteen, he was no match for the time-honored fraternity initiation of alcohol. At that moment his life started to unravel. By the time he was nineteen, it was clear that he was both a gifted intellect, actor, and athlete, and just as clear that his drinking was out of control.

It was ironic that Pop hadn't been drinking the night he

lost his leg. A member of the U.S. Lawn Tennis Association, he was returning home from a match with a carload of friends when a slow-moving train in the fog hit the car. Of the six people in the car, two died and the rest were badly injured. Pop's left foot was cut off, his right thigh and scalp were deeply gouged, and he suffered a massive loss of blood. Only his effort to walk over to help his friends—which jammed cinders and dirt into the leg wound, stemming the flow of blood saved his life.

For several days he lay in the hospital on the verge of death. If Pop's spirit was an accomplice in his initial survival, he soon regretted it. The whole city pulled for the injured teenager, a fact the *Richmond News Leader* reported under a huge page one headline, "Scherer Rallies." But lying in his hospital bed wracked with pain and reviewing the wreckage of his life, my father contemplated suicide.

Pop asked to borrow Granddaddy's pocketknife one evening, saying he just wanted to clean his fingernails. A knowing look passed between the two men. But my grandfather said, "Sure thing son, I'll see you in the morning." He handed over the knife and walked out the door. Pop said he wrestled all night long with that decision. In the end though, the power of his father's trust swayed him. And when Granddaddy returned in the morning all that he said was, "Glad to see you Son." They both knew what had happened, yet they never spoke of it.

So there you have a thumbnail sketch of the background that shaped me. Jesus might have loved me, as my grandfather liked to remind me, but my parents did not seem to want to raise me, which could only mean that there was something awfully wrong with me, a fact of which my stuttering was a daily reminder. When the U.S. Navy hired John Jacob Scherer IV, it got a man who tried, literally, with every breath, to compensate— often successfully—for some tragic insufficiency he knew was his.

It took a stormy sea and the desperate need of an aircrew in danger to bring out another me. In no way did I play a conscious role in the emergence of this new person, in the untying of the knots in my tongue and in my heart; something beyond me was clearly the author.

The above details I have disclosed in the spirit of going back to the blackboard and "showing my work" of reporting to you as best I can about where the convictions that shape me come from.

After my four years on EATON, I went on my way, which included graduating from seminary, serving as the Senior Pastor of the Lutheran Church of Ithaca, New York, and as chaplain of Cornell University, eventually leaving the parish ministry to help create a graduate program in the Applied Behavioral Sciences. That led to the establishment of the consulting practice that, for many years now, has allowed me to enjoy the company of some of the most interesting people in the country.

In the early seventies, I had the good fortune of stumbling across another path that would change my life in an unusual way, a path that would turn out to be as much a well of spiritual sustenance to me as my grandfather's special kind of Lutheran love was. The stage had been set for this to happen when my grandfather had said, shortly before he died: "I think the next big step in the religious world will be the coming together of the Eastern and Western spiritual paths."

That must have gone in deep, because some fifteen years later I found myself drawn to learn more about such an Eastern spiritual path. In fact, I have often wished Granddaddy could have met the people from the Kripalu Yoga Ashram. My exposure to this path began when my first wife and I divorced in 1973 and she moved from Ithaca with our five year old son, Jay, to become one of the first residents to live and study at the Ashram (the Indian word for spritual retreat), then located just outside Philadelphia in Sunnytown, Pennsylvania. When I would visit the two of them— as I often did—I felt a wonderful kind of peace. Not exactly like coming home, but something close, something familiar.

Most of the clients wore loose clothing, which made doing the yoga, a crucial part of their practice, easier. In the early

1970s these trappings put off many people, especially those raised in the Christian tradition like myself. But it never put me off. From the first meeting I experienced in my ex-wife and her new colleagues the deep humanity, the humble, loving acceptance, that is the hallmark of the world's greatest religions. Many of them—including my ex-wife—became close friends, and still are to this day.

If I were to summarize what they taught me, it would be how to infuse the spiritual practice of my faith into everything that I do. *Seva* is *Sadhana,* one of their fundamental principles, applies here. The phrase means: *daily work is a classroom for Spiritual development.* Everything that happens to us when we work, when held correctly, can be a contribution to our growing into who God knows us to be. In addition, every person and situation we meet becomes an opportunity for service, for giving of the highest and best of who we are, something Granddaddy would certainly have applauded.

I learned about three elements in the Eastern spiritual path: meditation (listening to the divine voice), physical stretches (which do a lot more than make you flexible), and an emphasis on service to others. All are aimed at engaging "The Witness," which you can only do by quieting the distractions of the mind. As long as the mind is agitated with though—which it is most of the time—it is virtually impossible to hear what God might be saying to you.

Perhaps what folks at the Ashram call "engaging The Witness," is what Jesus was referring to when he spoke of "entering the kingdom of God," which he also said was "within." In this kingdom, the rules of the road are reversed, where being first becomes losing, where what has been most important becomes least important, and where fear no longer controls your life. Sages throughout the centuries have called this state things like, the "higher self." St. Paul referred to it as "the Christ within me." I prefer to think of it as the Human Spirit—and we all have one.

Whatever you call it, our words describe a phenomenon of human experience that resides beyond what can be seen and measured. To acknowledge the existence of "The Witness" is to acknowledge that beyond the brain is some additional power of observation and choice.

Modern sciences offer tantalizing clues that there is an aspect to our lives that goes beyond our normal perceptions and preoccupations. For instance, a growing body of medical literature describes clinically documented examples of so called "near death experiences. Often, in these events, a person connected to sensitive instruments dies. The EKG goes flat, the heart stops, the glandular system ceases functioning, and brain activity is gone. Medical technicians work feverishly to restart the vital processes.

Meanwhile, in account after account, *all of this is being witnessed by the deceased.* People describe the sensation of floating out of their bodies and looking down on the recovery efforts from the emergency room ceiling. They talk of bright lights and sensations of overwhelming happiness, well-being, and love—joys too radiant to be reflected by the thin mirror of human language. And then there is a disorienting crash and they slam back into their bodies, reconnected again to the limited sensors of life. What actually happens during these episodes? Something. That's all we really know. To me, these experiences point to the possibility of a human spirit beyond our physical bodies.

From my colleagues at Kripalu, I learned a reliable means of experiencing the perspective of "The Witness." It doesn't require a near-death experience. It can be accessed all the time by someone who is awake and trained. It is the spiritual equivalent of launching a telescope into space—in this case inner space. For in perceiving our world we define it, and in perceiving it with the physical senses alone, we miss much of what is there. In our work with business leaders we call this practice "Centering," which, along with daily early morning yoga training, becomes an impor-tant, in some cases life saving, benefit of their intensive experience.

For me, yoga as a spiritual practice was an exhilarating discovery, offering a tool I had often wished for in the practice of my faith. Christianity, like all religions, is long on prescriptions for the external exercise of faith, admonitions of *what* to be in the world—loving, generous, patient, courageous, forgiving, etc. But on the question of *how* to cultivate the inner spiritual practices, which support these virtues, the mainstream religions, and even my theological training, were for the most part silent. Yoga, I discovered, is not a religion at all, but merely a methodology of experiencing the wholeness of oneself, for reintegrating the body, mind, and spirit. For me, "Centering" is a means of following the advice St. Paul gave to the Romans when he said, "Do not conform to this world, but instead be transformed by the renewal of your mind."

"Centering" distances the practitioner from the reflexive emotional responses to life's trials and tribulations. The more "centered" your habits of mind, the more you are able to experience fully the assault of daily experience and yet avoid conforming to this world with an automatic reaction, usually fear-based. You can instead select from a wider menu of responses, which are not usually "on the screen" of the human brain. Thus, yoga and meditation or "Centering" can be useful tools for the renewal of the mind. I'm surprised St. Paul himself didn't think to mention this.

From Granddaddy and my early days at the parsonage I saw how faith naturally expresses itself in the day-to-day activities of the world. From teachers and colleagues at the Ashram, I learned simple things to do on a daily basis to integrate the spirit in life and work. The influence of these two places shaped the program I designed for corporate leaders.

I found that with something as simple as breathing, it is possible to control your reactions and shift your interpretation of reality. I learned that what you want to change you shouldn't fight, because what we fight we make stronger. (I wish Pop had known this.) And I learned that work itself, far from being a necessary evil, can become a vehicle for spiritual growth. It became clear to me that by learning to recruit the assistance of the human spirit, pressure-worn executives could reclaim portions of their lives which tradition had taught must be sacrificed to the ruthless gods of success. They could also learn to lead and manage in ways more humane and effective than anything they had known so far.

4

The Program

WHEN EXECUTIVES AND THEIR SPOUSES arrive for their Executive Development Intensive (EDI), they are in effect keeping an appointment with themselves. The appointment covers (three-and-a-half days)—the best part of a work week. Before it begins, however, a month or two of preparation, "pre-work" we call it, has taken place. After the week in Spokane, there are up to two months of follow-up phone reviews. It adds up to an experience that encompasses a significant part of the year. With any luck at all—and we've been pretty lucky—it is a momentous episode for all concerned.

Most participants in the EDI have chosen freely to partake, having heard of it from a friend or colleague who went through. A few executives have been "sent." And occasionally a senior executive attends the program, then returns to the office and reccommends it to all directly reporting managers.

In any event, those who come for the program engage in a process that begins with the completion of a computer-assisted management assessment and development tool. We send enrollees two program disks containing a number of questions. Enrollees use one disk to do a self-assessment, and the other they gamely hand out to a minimum of four (and up to twelve) colleagues. The colleagues then respond, anonymously of course, to a similar questionnaire. The result is a great gift: a view of ourselves as others see us.

The questions, incidentally, assess subjects on how they deal with such matters as conflict, the exercise of power, helping others, openness to change, response to authority, etc. Many of the elements of the assessment correlate well with the inner work of the Intensive. And it gives participants a handy reference document they can take home with them in order to benchmark their progress in areas they choose to focus on.

In addition, enrollees are sent a written questionnaire, which, if conscientiously approached, will take three to four hours to answer. This material covers descriptions of important relationships in their lives (at home and at work), their physical health, eating habits, issues that concerns them on the job, etc. Most important, it queries them on what they wish to accomplish through their Intensive. With this information the team tailors the process to each individual.

The program staff consists of a pair of Core Facilitators; usually a man and a woman (to be matched with the same gender participant), exercise experts, a nutritionist, massage professional, and a yoga instructor.

Good Core Facilitators are hard to find. Those we draw on come from a very small group scattered from New York to Hawaii, and I would describe them as both spiritually grounded and fluent in the language of business. By that, I mean they actively cultivate a balanced life of the spirit, mind, and body, and they are also experienced with and sympathetic to the corporate world. It is an interesting combination of traits. Members of the faculty must be dedicated in their practices but relaxed about them too, completely non-dogmatic and respectful of the intensely personal nature of spirituality.

Participants usually arrive on a Sunday afternoon and are settled into a comfortable hotel room, where, for the next several days their undivided attention can be focused on their own inner work. Spouses receive the same program as the executives. There is some joint work, but most of the Intensive is individual.

Later in the afternoon, the couple meet with their facilitators. After the schedule is reviewed there is a preliminary discussion, based on the pre-work, about goals. Depending on how that discussion goes, the participants might be given some homework, asked to reflect on certain questions individually, or discuss something between themselves.

At six the next morning each participant is met at the hotel room by their own personal exercise coach. For thirty to forty-five minutes they will engage in the physical activity of their choice—walking, jogging, aerobics, biking, swimming, weight training (we even had someone do Tai Chi recently) —whatever they want to do, so long as they move their bodies and breathe the good air. Next, they do thirty to forty minutes of yoga with the yoga instructor. This offers a chance to stretch, cool down, relax, to "soften" and prepare for the work of the day. After that they shower and have breakfast on their own. The facilitators come calling at precisely nine in the morning, and off they go for one-on-one sessions. The adventure has now truly begun.

Each day has a theme or inquiry, which generates the grist for the conversations. Day One: *Why are you here?* Day Two: *What's been running your life?* Day Three: *What's a purpose worthy of who you are?* Day Four: *Who/What needs to be faced?* Added together, they reconnect work and the human spirit.

One approach that often proves to be quite powerful for this purpose is the use of the "Onion Model" so named because it helps people peel away the reasons behind their actions. Typically, they discover that the "self" they have been selling to the world is a façade. Behind the facade is a fear of some kind, usually based on a very old perception of threat or danger, and behind the fear is a "Formula for Success." A more blunt way to think of this formula is as a con game. Formulas for Success, "the Con," involve the specific steps we take in order to erect the facade we consider necessary for happiness, prosperity, survival, and love.

We draw all of this on an easel, because it makes visible the patterns that control us. Once people have identified this formula—their Con—they are invited to consider its purpose whether it is worthy of the energies of their life. We ask people if the Con is taking them where they want to go. Rarely is the answer yes.

Typically, lunch on the first day and then one other meal are spent with a nutritionist. Following lunch, bodywork begins. We consider the bodywork to be crucial, based on the following assumptions.

1. Body, mind, and spirit are a continuum.

2. The body is one of the most direct avenues to the human spirit.

3. The body is a metaphor for the Con game which the mind, left to its own devices, usually plays on the world.

4. It's also the best way we know to transcend the limitations of the mind.

After that, the first day's work is concluded. Not surprisingly, most people feel wrung out. They also report considerable feelings of confusion, as though something inside them had started to come loose.

The following days are a repeat, with variations, of the first.

During the facilitation of the second day, people often do "double chair work," in which they have imaginary conversations with others, living or dead, who are or were significant in their lives. Paragons of rationality, many executives can at first have a hard time with such role-playing. By now, however, they have seen that much of what passes for reality is up for grabs. With few exceptions, they invest themselves fully in this exercise. The dividends are priceless. At the end of the second day, participants glimpse ways of getting beyond their facade, of literally *being* some new way in the world.

Almost unfailingly on the third day, perhaps the most intense day of their professional lives, Intensive participants decide to embrace a new purpose. Actually, it's more like *receiving* a new purpose. For by now they have become a highly attentive witness to the way they have been living, and the result of that witnessing automatically brings a shift.

On the last day, with a new set of possibilities clearly defined, participants draw up a plan of action, a concrete set of commitments by which they will address those possibilities and continuously probe for new ones.

That doesn't seem such an exotic process. Still, it is one that has produced real change in people's lives, more lives, we are told, than just those who have gone through the program. These changes were spurred by nothing more than a moment in time, a moment when something old and painful was transformed into something with greater possibility.

The Stories

5

Shell

"Showing Dad" for Fifty Years

SHELL USUALLY GOT EVERYTHING HE WANTED. He told me that in virtually every meeting he attended he walked out with the decision he hoped for. He was on a fast track to the top of his organization, a "water-walker" as people said, destined to one day be president of this or some other company in the industry.

As we talked during his Intensive, he recounted the tricks he had mastered to win people over to his way of thinking. "I have perfected the repertoire," he said. "I use charm and well rehearsed communication skills. Sometimes I even use veiled threats of dire consequences to the company or our division if we don't do what I'm proposing. Also, over the years I've developed a network of relationships with key people throughout the company. People have told me that I'm persuasive, but what they may not know is that it's because I have a great drive for results."

His colleagues indicated that as a result of all this, he was a formidable opponent in a fight, and few people had the courage to take him on.

"So, what's the problem?" I asked.

"The problem is that I leave every meeting with a bad taste in my mouth. Lately, I've also had an upset stomach. I'll get what I wanted, and I'll think, 'I pulled it off again.' I'm not getting the satisfaction or the peace of mind I ought to. I'm stressed all the time, waiting for the house of cards to come crashing down around me. In meetings, I can feel my heart pounding when it seems like something isn't going the way I want. I'll probably die before I figure out how to not *have to* get what I want all the time."

"Can you think of a time when you didn't have that pressure inside you to make sure you got what you were after?"

Shell thought for a long time.

"Yes. . . I can see myself as a little kid, riding my bike around the neighborhood and wearing a cowboy hat and two six guns. What a delight! Nothing to prove. It was just fun to do things." He smiled wistfully.

"So when did it change?"

"Oh, yeah. . . I remember the day like it was yesterday. I was six or seven and I was playing in the sandbox beside our house. I had been building this scene—it was more than just buckets of sand shaped into towers and walls, we're talking an entire city, with streets, buildings, with bridges, everything. I'd been working on it for several days. My father was a big businessman, CEO of his company, and he had been gone. I couldn't wait for him to come home so I could show him what I had built.

"I was in the sandbox when his car drove up. I got so excited. I said, "Look, Dad! Look what I've built!" He stared at the creation for a moment and made a disgusted kind of sound like, 'Oh, brother!' Then he said, 'Well, you're probably going to turn out to be a ditch digger!' And he went into the house.

"I was crushed. I remember feeling sad—I cried for a while—and then I got mad. I must have said something to myself like, 'I'll show *him*!'" Shell paused.

"I guess I'm still trying to show him." His eyes became wet. "And he's been dead for years. When will I be able to stop?"

"How much is it costing you to operate this way?" I asked after awhile. "Or is it working for you? You're doing great things and everybody respects you. People are willing to take a cut in pay to transfer to your unit. What's the problem?"

"Like I said, I'm tired of *having to* walk on water all the time! It's killing me. . ."

"Would you like to find a way to work hard and succeed without *having* to?"

"Are you kidding?" Shell was skeptical. "You bet. But I don't think it's possible. I haven't been able to stop all these years."

Because the conversation he should have had with his father was still living inside him, I invited Shell to speak to his father now.

"But he's dead! How can I resolve it with him now?" He agreed to imagine his father was still alive.

"Dad..." he began, but had to stop as the tears came. "Dad, why did you say that to me? Why did you put me down like that?"

Then Shell imagined he was his own father.

"Son," he said, "I don't know *why* I said that to you. That city you built in the sandbox really was quite a remarkable piece of work. I told many of my friends about it afterward, bragging about you. Maybe I was just crabby from work or something. Heck, I don't know. I'm sorry it hit you so hard. I sure didn't intend *that*."

As Shell became himself again, he responded to his father. "It turns out I've been trying to compensate for that all my life, Dad, trying to get your approval, your love. I feel like I never did get it, even with all the success I had in school, in sports, in business." The anger was rising and Shell's voice became hard. "It was like I was never enough for you. What will it take for you to just love me, approve of me? That's all I want." He cried again.

After a few minutes he was breathing normally. His father had something more to say.

"Son, I do love you, I did love you—a lot. I just didn't know how to show it. I'm so sorry it ended up with you not knowing how much respect I had for you. You have been a wonderful son and I am very proud of you."

"Yes, but would you love me if I failed at something? If I got fired or left the business?"

"You bet I would! I failed several times in my life as you know. It's no big thing; you just pick yourself up and keep on going."

I asked Shell if he could let go of the resentment and hurt he had suffered from his father's unintentional cruelty.

He spoke directly to his father from his heart. "Dad, I love you and I forgive you for what you did to me. I understand that you were frustrated and distracted in your own life. I'm sorry that I blamed you all these years, too."

When he was finished, Shell wondered if this little exercise could possibly heal all the hurt feelings he had carried his whole life. After a few moments of reflection, he smiled hesitantly and said, "I feel something inside. It's as if something heavy is gone...I feel lighter. It's like he was really *here* in this room and something really did get resolved. This is amazing! I wonder if it is real, though."

It wasn't exactly an instantaneous cure. The key for Shell was to be able to catch himself operating out of that same prove-it-to-Dad place and gently forgiving himself and his father, again and again. The voice that had been driving him to impress his father gradually faded.

Shell told me the other day, "I may not be president, but I definitely am having more fun, getting even more done and just enjoying the heck out of what I'm doing. That old feeling of pressure to achieve only comes over me once in awhile, and I know where it's coming from when it does."

"What do you do then?" I asked.

"I thank that voice for being concerned and then I say, 'I love you; it's okay. Come on ahead. We'll be all right.' It sounds strange, but it really works! I realized that the way I was going, I would never be able to relax, and never be able to 'get there,' since it was actually myself, not Dad, who had to be convinced I was worth something. I feel like that old Joan Baez folk song that says, 'I have been released.'"

6

Brenda

Crossing Over to Safety

BRENDA CAME WILLINGLY enough to her Executive Development Intensive. She just wasn't exactly sure why she was there. Her boss, whom she respected a great deal, had said, "I think this is something you might find valuable. Why don't you check it out." So she came, bright, alive, energetic, articulate, full of ideas and, by her own report, stubborn. At one point on the first day we got around to this question:

"Where are you experiencing challenge or difficulty at work?" After some thought, she answered, "With Charlie."

"What's the problem?"

"Well, I don't know how to explain it. He's just kind of... I mean we never seem to be able to..." She paused, stumped as to how to describe the situation.

I asked her to imagine Charlie sitting in the room. What would she say to him to clear the air? Her reaction was almost violent.

"What? Are you kidding?" Sit here and talk to an empty chair? That's the dumbest thing I've ever heard. . . Absurd!"

"What's this strong reaction about? What would happen if you carried on an imaginary conversation with Charlie?"

"I don't know what would happen if I did!" she replied after a long pause.

"Is that what's stopping you?"

"Yes. . . I have to know exactly what will happen before I'll do anything. And if I start talking to Charlie in an empty chair—which I will never do—I don't know what might come out. I don't want to find out, and I certainly don't want *you* to find out, at least not until I've had a chance to smooth it out a little."

"So what would happen if you *don't* talk to the empty chair?" I asked. "Does that seem more predictable?"

"Well, no, now that I think about it, it really doesn't. I don't really know what would happen next if I don't do what you are asking, but I would feel better if I didn't."

By this time, she was getting irritated. "Look, what has this got to do with me and my management effectiveness?"

"Maybe nothing," I confessed. "But you seem to have a *lot* of energy about not losing control and about not doing anything unless you believe you can see the outcome clearly. Is that what you're saying?"

"Sure! You don't get anywhere in my organization by not knowing where you're headed!"

"Where are you headed here in this Intensive?" I asked. "Maybe there's a clue there."

Long pause again. "Well, I get a lot done, and done well,

but I've been told that I am hard to work with sometimes, that I give the impression that I could do whatever needs to be done better than anybody else—and that I'm usually right about that. I may be too smart for my own good."

"So, what's the problem?"

Brenda reflected for a few minutes on what the consequences might be if she trusted people. She noticed she had a funny feeling. It seemed like she felt frightened. But she wasn't the only stubborn person in the room.

"Okay, let's take another run at it... There's Charlie, sitting over there in that chair. What do you need to say to him?"

"There you go again! I'm *not* going to talk to Charlie!"

"Okay, how about imagining *me* in the chair and tell me what a dumb idea this is. . .?"

"You can't be serious. If I won't put *Charlie* in the chair, what makes you think I'll put *you* there?"

"I don't really care *who* you put there, or if you never put *anyone* there. My commitment is to your uncovering and getting beyond the fear of trying something you can't control."

"I'm afraid—all right? I'm just afraid... When I can't see how something is going to turn out, I get a little afraid."

After a long beat: "What might be a benefit to you—at work—if you *weren't* afraid when the future wasn't predictable?"

She raised her eyebrows and looked up.

"I might get more done. It takes me a long time to move on things that have components that I can't foresee . . . My people might feel more respected; I can see where they get that I don't really trust them . . . I would sure feel more relaxed. I'm tight all the time."

Would she be willing to try something new, even though she was afraid?

"That's not logical . . ."

Correct. Would she be willing to do something that's not logical but that might benefit her in a way that couldn't be predicted?

"That's *definitely* not logical!"

True. She could leave the room this minute, go outside, walk around Riverfront Park. She could be all alone. It was her choice.

I can't tell you how long the pause was as Brenda wrestled with her internal dialogue between the fear, which she knew, had no real basis in reality, and her desire for a breakthrough. Of course, by now she saw that it was much more than just talking to the chair. Those three degrees of arc between aiming her vocal chords at the empty chair and continuing to aim them at me had come to represent all the things she had chosen not to do in her life out of deference to her fear.

"I've got to do this," she said with emotion.

Of course, she didn't have to. She could maintain the feeling of safety, which was so important to her. But she wondered what might happen if she didn't live each moment in fear of being in the land of the unknown.

She finally said, "I'd have *life*. . ." and she began to cry freely.

After several minutes, she looked up and said, "Okay, here I go . . ."

She slid forward to the edge of the sofa and stared at the chair only a few feet away. You could see the turmoil working inside her as she confronted herself, faced her fear.

Her voice cracked as she began. "Okay, Charlie, it's taken me awhile to get here, but now that I'm talking to you, here's what it's been like lately working with you. . ."

She stopped, looked at me, and a slow smile of triumph appeared across her face. She jumped up, let out a "WHOOP!" and virtually danced around the room.

"Wow!" she said with a mix of wonder and excitement. "This feels great! Amazing! Here I am . . . I did it! It was not logical—it was absurd actually—but I did it anyway and something big happened inside myself! I'm on the other side of fear! Jeez, what a feeling . . . I feel energized like I haven't in a long time. I want to run or write something or do something. Whew!"

In the little skit we had contrived, Brenda said hardly a word to Charlie. She realized she didn't have to. Her relationship with Charlie really didn't matter. After a few minutes, she spoke of all the places where she stopped herself—and maybe even her team—whenever things looked like they might get beyond what she was familiar with. Being fast and smart, that didn't happen often, but *she* knew when those moments were. She said it was like "being set free." Some kind of powerful unleashing had just occurred for Brenda.

A week or so after the EDI was over, her boss called. "What did you do to Brenda?" he demanded. I hate those questions. I didn't know if he was mad or not. So I didn't say anything. "She's become a whirlwind of effectiveness since she got back. She was always a star performer, but now she's even more amazing. And she seems to be enjoying herself, not so uptight all the time."

The other day I had an opportunity to speak to Brenda about including her experience in the book, and I asked her if the breakthrough she had in her Intensive had stuck. "You bet," she said, "Not a day goes by that I don't step through that same door about something, dragging my fear and logic with me. Those two are not protesting as loudly as before, either. I think we're all starting to believe that we might actually be safe."

7

Frantz

Discovering the New World of Choice

FRANTZ WAS SENT TO HIS INTENSIVE. That's the only way to say it. His older European cousin, Carl, who ran the company and its plants in twelve countries around the world, had told him in no uncertain terms to get himself sorted out. "Try that program in Spokane," he had said to Frantz. "Then let's talk."

Prior to the Intensive, Carl briefed me by saying that Frantz was in over his head and that he, Carl, was partly to blame. "My father and his father are brothers, and, as a favor to them before they retired, I agreed to place Frantz in a field position where he could get some real world management experience. I sent him to South America as the production manager. Production is failing miserably there. His work isn't effective, but no one will tell me to my face."

"Why not?" I asked. "Well, the main issue is that we have the same last name! Everybody knows that I put him there and that he's my younger cousin. So people are very reluctant to tell me what's going on, even the other senior managers, including the on-site president. All I know is that our numbers are down and he's in charge of production."

When Carl reflected on what might be the ideal outcome

of Frantz's Intensive, he said, "I want whatever is best for Frantz."

"No matter what that looks like?"

"Yes. No matter what it looks like. I want him to succeed in his work, just as if he were my brother. But I want him to be happy. His father will be upset with me, and certainly with Frantz, if he fails where he is. He's hoping that Frantz will become a senior director with the company. He asks me how he's doing all the time. I'm feeling a lot of pressure. If you can do it, please help Frantz be a better manager, for him and for the company."

"Okay, Carl, but you know how we work: the goals that matter are the ones set by the participant. Does he know the stakes are high from your point of view?"

"Yes, I have told him. He's under tremendous pressure now, from me, from his own numbers and, I'm sure, from his father."

Before his arrival, Frantz had several conversations with me as a part of the pre-work, to focus on why he was coming. His homework was to arrive ready to go to work on a specific goal that was his, not someone else's. He and his wife, Katerina, arrived and we began.

Toward the end of the first day I asked him how things were going at work.

"Well, not bad, really. I'm having some growing pains, I think you call them, but everything is under control."

"But I understand from what you tell me—and Carl says the same thing—that production is *way* off and doesn't seem likely to come around any time soon."

"Yes, well, we have some major problems in the economy, you see, with major inflation. This makes it very hard for us."

"In production? How does this keep production down?"

I wasn't buying it, and he knew it. "John, this is hard to say." He looked down at the floor. "I'm . . . I'm failing . . ."

He was visibly upset.

"I'm really failing and I don't know what to do . . .Why did they put me in this position? This is the first real job I've had in my entire life! I worked while I was in school in part-time summer positions and the like, but I've never had a job before with real responsibility. I've been a graduate student for the past five years . . . I'm only 26 and now they make me production manager in another country, where the last person to have the job left with a nervous breakdown! I don't know anything about *production*, for God's sake . . . I'm an *architect*! But there's no place for an architect in our company."

He had accepted the job to please his father, but of course, his father wasn't especially pleased at the way things were going. Despite the difficulties of being ill suited for the work and unhappy, Frantz didn't see any way out of his current downward spiral. He felt that if he didn't succeed his father would be terribly disappointed and angry. But even in his wildest dreams, Frantz couldn't imagine himself succeeding in his present position. In his mind he had two choices—he could ask to be transferred home, admitting he had failed in South America, or he could stay on and keep trying to make it work. The second choice was punctuated by his assertion that under no circumstances could he even envision being a successful production manager.

The turning point came when he contemplated a mystical possibility. If he could have anything he wanted, something to make his heart sing, something closer to who he really was, if he could have it without guilt or being wrong for wanting it, what would he want to be doing?

His face looked very sad. "I don't know what I would really want to do with my life . . . I've always done whatever my father, or my uncle, or lately what Katerina wanted me to do. Isn't that pathetic?"

As he searched his imagination and his heart, he tripped upon a new idea. "Perhaps I could be some kind of consultant to help people. What I know the most about is architecture and a little engineering. Maybe I could get a position somewhere helping other organizations in those two areas. But . . . my father would never buy it. There's not enough security in it, and it's not the family business."

"So, you have no choice, really . . ."

"No, I don't."

"If you *did* have a choice—I understand that you don't— what would you choose for yourself?"

"If I did have a choice?" Then his face lit up. He sat up on the edge of his chair. "I would ask Carl to be released from my present position, but not suddenly. I have a few things that I have put in place, based on some engineering principles, which I believe could help the production problems. I'd like to see them given a chance. Then I would tell my father how grateful I have been for his support and all the opportunities he has created for me, but that I was choosing a different direction for myself from the one he chose for me."

He had a big smile.

"Yes, I can see him now . . . He would be disappointed, but, you know, he would also be surprised and proud of me, I believe. For taking a stand. He's never seen me do that."

"And how would *you* feel about yourself?"

Huge smile now. "Great! I'd feel great! Like a new lease on life, as you say."

Being that this conversation was hypothetical, based on a shaky, "if," *if* Frantz had any choice in the matter, it couldn't go very far until Frantz took a look at what constitutes having choices in a person's life. He might have been having trouble as a production manager, but he was brilliant at puzzling out a new paradigm or reality for himself.

"Choice doesn't come from other people giving it to you," I mused. "It doesn't come from fate or chance, does it? That would be too much to take. Maybe it comes from inside you."

" Yes, that's it! It comes from inside."

To have more choice for himself, he noted, would take a lot of courage. "I mean to hold off all the people who have their own agendas for me."

"Would you be willing to have choice and courage in your life, even if you don't know where they come from?" I asked him.

"That's a strange question...But, yes, I'd be willing to have them, even if I don't know where they come from and even if I haven't had them very often." He spoke with great strength and conviction.

"Okay, Frantz," I said, "Ready... Get set... Go!"

He laughed, "Oh, I get it! It's like Dorothy and the Tin Man and the Lion and the Wizard of Oz... I already have choice and courage... I just have to recognize that I do—and live as if they are there." The mist parted. He saw a new reality—it isn't that just a few people have courage and choice and other people don't. You have a choice by choosing. You have courage by feeling afraid and doing something anyway, bringing your fear with you into the experience.

"But I don't want to disappoint my father…"

"Of course you don't. You want him to be proud of you."

"Because I love him." His eyes filled with tears. He had been living his life guided by his desire to please his father. He wondered what would happen now.

"And your father's been helping you all these years because of his love for you," I pointed out. "Why does he give you so much advice, Frantz?"

"He doesn't think I can do it alone, I think."

"Do what?"

"Live my life…"

"Let me see if I got this. He loves you a lot and he doesn't trust you to live your life without his help, so he gives you a lot of help. Is that it?"

Pause. "Yes…But it sounds different now that you say it that way."

"What do you *wish* he would do with his love for you, Frantz?"

"I wish he would let go, let me have my own life. Let me succeed or fail by myself. But he wants me to succeed so badly…"

"Would you say that you are succeeding the way things are now? Are you making him happy?"

He chuckled. "No. That's easy… He's not happy at all

with me and what I've done with my life." It occurred to Frantz that he wasn't responsible for making his father happy.

"So, if you are failing now to make your father happy, and couldn't anyway, even if you did exactly what he wanted you to do, and if choice and courage come to people who exercise them, what are you going to do?

"Well, I could keep on trying... That's no good... I guess I could choose something for myself because I wanted to do it, and deal with his disappointment..."

"It sounds like you already have his disappointment to deal with!"

"Yes, that's right. So I don't really change him any... Just myself!"

"He already seems more relaxed to me." Katerina said from across the room. I could see what was happening, but he would just get mad whenever I said anything about it to him. What a relief to have him ready to make decisions for himself!"

"I am going to write my father a letter," Frantz said. "I started it already in my mind. I'll tell him how much I have appreciated his love over the years and how I am deciding to look for a job which is closer to my heart. Then I will send a similar letter to Carl, asking to be transitioned out of my current position. Then I am going to contact several engineering and consulting firms I know back home and throw my hat in the ring."

He sat calmly with a smile a mile wide on his face.

"Are you afraid?" I asked.

"A little...But I am more afraid of not doing what I know I must."

When I last heard from Frantz, he was a consulting engineer working for an engine manufacturer, going out to help their customers solve problems. He said life was not without difficulties, but that he and Katerina were expecting their first child and the he was enjoying his work, even the difficulties, for the first time in his life. "It's as if I wasn't even living before," he said. "I would rather be facing real problems awake than be facing them asleep, or, even worse, to be protected from facing them at all."

8

Rachel

The "Ice Queen" Thaws

RACHEL WAS ONE OF THE BEST AND THE BRIGHTEST managers at her Fortune 500 company. Her remarkable mind dominated her management style. With a lightning fast intellect, she could soak up details and make quick, accurate assessments. So it wasn't surprising she saw no need to bring her emotions to work at all.

But the truth was as she told us a year after her Intensive, "I had reached a very intellectual state. I lived most of my life in my head and very little in my feelings. I had lost contact with my real self."

It was ironic that Rachel felt comfortable in coming for her Intensive. The reason was that the computer score of her pre-work had squared perfectly with her self-image. She *knew* she was a task-oriented individual who wouldn't be slowed down by the baggage of feelings, and that's just what her score suggested. Rachel also knew that people considered her a hard person, an "ice queen." This wasn't an identity that she enjoyed, but she recognized the woman sketched in her assessment results, and the image, intimidating though it was, reassured her. "For someone, who was so in her mind, it was important to be predictable," she explained.

What Rachel ultimately experienced was a good illustration of how the body somehow preserves the integrity of the spirit, long after the toughness of the mind and its concepts have abandoned the spirit by the side of the road. It was during the bodywork portion of her Intensive that the sensations of long-forgotten issues began returning. Rachel says that while she didn't particularly care for the yoga, it nevertheless carried with it a "trance-like state" that caused her, quite unexpectedly, to be "hit by some very, very old issues."

At a crucial time in her life, Rachel suddenly remembered, she had needed her father's support. It wasn't there. During yoga on the second morning, she remembered that period in metaphorical imagery.

"I was on a journey. I saw myself moving through a very long tunnel, and it came to a stream. There was a waterfall at the end. I had to go over the waterfall. I was a little girl and I needed my father to help me over it, and he couldn't."

In a flash Rachel realized that in a long-forgotten moment of her girlhood she had put her feelings away.

"Where?" I asked her.

"Just away," she answered. "It was too painful for me to feel. So I just decided it was easier not to."

In a quiet moment in Spokane it all came back to her.

"I spent five straight days crying at the Intensive. Brian (her husband, also having his own Intensive) was as high as a kite.

things went wrong on that trip. I have no doubt that they were there on purpose. All kinds of little misunderstandings, one right after the other. Making arrangements that I thought were going to happen one way and they didn't work out that way. I ordered something for lunch and the wrong thing came. A lot of little aggravations. They just broke me down. I really did feel like there were spirits or something working for me those five days, trying to get me to a state where I had to let go. It got me to an emotional state I needed to get at. It got me out of my head...all those nagging things that seemed to say, 'All right, you have to feel this now. You're getting used to the nerve.'"

When Rachel went back to work, it was painfully obvious to her what had been happening throughout her career. Basically she had been managing with only part of herself. "I was missing the other piece," she said. The part of her that could feel, *that* part had never been allowed in the office. No wonder colleagues and subordinates saw her as hard.

So Rachel decided to change. It is easy to think that the way she changed was minor. We all have feelings, and she had simply decided to start experiencing hers. Big deal. Plus, she also decided to start factoring them into the mix of resources available to her as a manager.

What she soon experienced, though, was that the ability to feel and be guided by feeling is a very big deal.

Rachel's company is one of those giant institutions now going through downsizing and re-engineering. On paper those words—downsizing, re-engineering—seem precise and tidy. The reality they describe, however, is a whirlpool of pain and confusion. In the midst of it, organizations must achieve new vision and new community if they are to survive.

Rachel reports that bringing the caring part of her back to work is producing new levels of commitment and effort from those she works with.

"There is no question that learning to balance feeling and thinking has made me more effective as a manager," Rachel says. "Balance is the key, not to be overly emotional or overly intellectual. That's what makes good decisions. Building teamwork has become critical to the future of our company, and you can't do that if you're not sensitive to individual needs. I've learned to pay attention to the tone of people's voices, to the expression in people's faces and say, 'You know, you don't look like you're feeling right about this. Talk to me about what's really going on.'"

"I'm seeing that open honesty creates such a different organization. There's so much valuable information in people's body language and expressions. Learning to feel when something's not right with someone and clearing it up right away tends to bring out the best in them, individually and in their contribution to the team."

Rachel says that the rapid changes now re-shaping her company sometimes contribute to a negative atmosphere. Even so, her colleagues more and more are telling her that they feel lucky to work with her because of the caring she brings. It is a message she never used to hear.

"It's saying a lot for me that I've been able to get that feeling part back." Rachel describes how reconnecting with her emotions has also enhanced her ability to exercise executive authority. Wielding authority, *per se*, was never something she had a problem with.

"Before, if someone wasn't performing, I just said, 'Get rid of them. I don't have time for this.' Now I listen. I just listen. Some people are very smart, some less so, some maladjusted, etc. But everyone has something to contribute. I'm learning to help people discover where they can make their best contributions and to support them in doing that."

When confrontation is necessary, Rachel's feelings are helping her handle that better, too. Three subordinates recently "did something nasty," something, which in the past she would have treated as a purely disciplinary issue. This time she acknowledged to herself that, "I was really upset. I pulled them into an office immediately and said, 'You know something? I've got a problem with the three of you. You just did something that really hurt my feelings...' They knew exactly where I was coming from. They weren't surprised."

Clean as a whistle, the matter was handled. Similarly, at a "huge national accounts meeting" recently, a colleague gave a representation during which he blatantly, for political reasons, misrepresented information.

"I couldn't control myself," says Rachel. "In front of the whole group, I said, 'That is totally inaccurate. This is what the truth is...' The group started clapping and people came up to me afterward and thanked me for my honesty. Before, I wouldn't have allowed myself to feel my outrage, and I would have just swallowed it."

Rachel's new communion with her feelings is also allowing her to bring off one of the most difficult balancing acts of modern executive life.

"I am a much better mother now," she says. "Since the EDI, since starting to let myself feel my feelings, I no longer work twelve hours a day. It's important to me to be a good mother. I work nine to five and I don't let myself feel guilty about not working longer. My family is my priority, and I come in late when I have to and leave early when I have to. And when I'm at work, I don't let myself feel guilty about not being with my family. The elimination of guilt has made me so much more effective in both places. It's like going on vacation—you always get more done the week before you leave. It's the same type of thing. If you know that you only have these eight hours, you can get ten hours of work done. Living with my feelings has allowed me to be much more focused. When I'm at work, I'm at work. When I'm home, I'm home."

9

Sandy

From Being Tolerated to Being a Partner

SANDY WAS A FAST-TRACKER, receiving promotions before his peers and serving in a new position in the international division of his large engineering and manufacturing company. He had a ready wit and knew a lot about many subjects, from baseball to nuclear physics.

During his moments of deep reflection, he described the facade he presented to himself and the rest of the world.

"I want to be bright and witty and strong... To be seen as caring about people and what happens. Knowledgeable—about *everything* actually. I don't want to be caught without something important to say on any subject under discussion. And that's at home as well as at work."

He realized this front was created so that he would feel useful to other people. His fear was that people might find out, "... that sometimes I don't know what the heck I'm talking about. And that sometimes I really don't give a rip. Oh, and that sometimes I carry around a holier-than-thou attitude, feeling superior to everyone else."

Underneath it all, Sandy didn't want people to know that he needed them.

"What's the fear?" I asked him. "What happens to someone who doesn't know what they are talking about, doesn't really care, feels superior to everybody else, but in reality needs them?"

He thought for a long time.

"They are shunned. They get left out. Nobody wants to be with them."

We had hit The Fear. Everybody has one. It's usually some variation of what Sandy's was; fear of rejection, abandonment, or being unloved. And it's what drives much of our thinking and behavior, even our successes.

Early in life we all discovered that we were not okay as we were, that we had to be different or be like somebody else to be worthy of love and acceptance: smarter, bigger, better looking, faster. Something, we come to believe, is wrong with us or missing. We develop a masterful strategy for compensating for that "flaw" which makes us unacceptable as we are. This strategy becomes a way of life for us, an unconscious belief system that underlies everything we say and do; it even underlies what we think. We don't have it like a thought; *it has us*. Soon it has turned into a habitual pattern, complete with thoughts, feelings, behaviors, sometimes even a posture, to go with it. After awhile we come to believe that this character is who we *are*.

When Sandy looked at his Formula for Success in life, he

realized that he wanted to be useful, persuasive, bright, and knowledgeable.

"Why I asked?"

"Using this strategy," he said, "the best possible outcome is that people will tolerate me... God, I hate that. That's the way I feel a lot of the time—tolerated. Can you believe it? I'm trying to achieve minimal disdain. And the best I can get is zero disdain; I rarely feel I'm in the plus zone."

Of course, every strategy has some payoffs. For Sandy, he felt safe behind his facade. "I get to avoid the risks of ever getting close to people—and being vulnerable. Another thing is predictability; I usually know how things will turn out. I know people will eventually respect and tolerate me. Then, too, I guess it has brought me a certain amount of success; I've had some great jobs in the company and I'm told that I am a strong contributor."

"Operating this way gives me a feeling—it's an illusion, I know—of strength and control..."

"Is that it? Anything else a part of the payoff?"

"No, that's about it. Boy, that's not a pretty picture, is it?

"Well," I said, "it's working, isn't it? I mean within certain limits. It's brought you this far."

"Yeah, but it doesn't feel very good now, seeing it so clearly. As a matter of fact, now that I think about it, it doesn't feel all that good when I'm doing it!"

On the flip side of this strategy were some consequences. He ticked them off on his fingers, one by one.

"I've already said it costs me intimacy. That seems like both a cost and a payoff to me now. I don't have many close friends. And the friends I do have—well, we don't really talk about anything important, I mean personal. Also, I can't relax. I've always got to be on guard. You know, I have to be right all the time, thinking fast about what's going on to make sure I'm on top of everything, got the answer—or at least got *an* answer. It's tiring..."

"And I guess I'm always manipulating people to try to get them to tolerate me, to prove myself to them. I didn't see that before. There's a lot of stress in that position, I'll tell you! I think I've also started to lose my sense of who I really am."

"So," I said, "let me summarize bluntly, maybe even exaggerate to drive it home. Your operating purpose in life has been to get people to respect you, no *tolerate* you, by being so smart and indispensable to them that they *have* to use you, in spite of their basic dislike for you. And underneath it all, you have disdain for them and feel somehow superior. Is that it?"

"Man, that's hard to look at. But it feels right to me, and good to get it out on the table where I can see it."

"Sandy, is that purpose in life—to get people to tolerate you—worthy of who you are? Is that purpose sufficient for you?

"Never. No way…It's disgusting, actually."

"So, if you could somehow re-program yourself with a new purpose, one that might be closer to who you really are underneath all this habitual inner talk, what might that purpose accomplish for you? What could life be like with a new purpose?"

He smiled. "It might allow me to relax, enjoy my work and my life, get closer to people, let me be wrong from time to time, and to need people. I would trust more, be a partner rather than a competitor all the time over who's contributing the most, or has the best answer."

I asked him if he'd ever had an experience like that.

"Yes! Not long ago I was sent into a situation where I had to work side-by-side with another manager—it's complicated organizationally, but we were, in effect, equals. I was told by Corporate to work together with him. Theo had been there for a long while and knew the ropes, so when I came in, I asked him if he would help me, *teach* me, really. He was great. He showed me everything he knew little things he didn't have to tell me about but which were very helpful. When we had a problem, either one of us, we always told each other about it and worked on it together. We argued, sometimes with a lot of heat, but I knew that it was all about getting to the best solution and I didn't take it personally. I trusted him and he trusted me."

"How would you sum up your relationship?"

"We were…were…*partners*."

Sandy's eyes got wet. "We were *partners,*" he said gently, as though he were in awe of an important discovery.

"Did you have to get Theo to tolerate you?" I asked

"Nope. I just asked him to help me and offered my help to him."

"Did he tolerate you?"

He laughed at the absurdity of the question. "Yes! He more than tolerated me; he trusted me. You know—this is an awkward thing to say about a business buddy—but I would have to say that we loved each other. I mean, we really trusted each other and were there for each other and didn't have to wonder whether the other one was going to 'get' you. You know what I mean?"

When Sandy looked at what was different about this situation, he realized that it started out in an unusual way. "Now that I think about it, asking for help was the exact opposite of my Formula for Success, as you call it."

"So, if your purpose with him was not to impress him, what was it?"

"Just to work with him and do my best. To be his partner."

"If you *had* another purpose, a new one, what would it be?" I asked him. "Why are you on this planet if it's not to manipulate people into tolerating you? Maybe there's a clue in your relationship with Theo."

He said he'd think about it overnight. The next morning I asked him what he came up with. He said he wasn't sure but was willing to try something new to find another purpose. He meditated for several minutes. With his eyes closed, relaxed, letting go of his usual thoughts, he did nothing more than notice his breath.

"What is your real purpose for being here?" I asked quietly. "Don't even try to answer the question. Just let it drift through your mind and see what comes."

A slow smile appeared. His voice caught in his throat.

"I know," he said quietly. "I know what I'm here to do. *I am to be effective through the grace of others.*"

This last was said with power and force and certainty. I was reminded of a martial arts master focused enough to split bricks. All of a sudden, Sandy was different. The nervous energy, which used to characterize him, was gone. His eyes were steady and clear; he wasn't reacting to what was happening.

"You know," he said, "those words seemed to come from another place, not my mind. They just came to me. I was actually surprised when I heard them come out, like I was hearing myself speak, rather than thinking it up. Weird. It took my breath away. My heart started beating faster. It scared me a little and excited me at the same time. If this *could* be me, what a difference it would make in my effectiveness—in my life!"

"What could you do right away to begin living out of your new strategy?" I asked.

"Well, first thing... I think I will invite my new boss, my new team, and my new colleagues to help me and my department, to be our partners and teachers in what we have to do. That'll shock a bunch of people right there!"

"What do you think their response will be?"

"Oh, I think they'll really like it! They complain all the time about how we haven't been helping them, haven't been team players. If we ask them to help us, they can't complain so much, can they? How can they be against our proposing to be partners, for Pete's sake? I think this will work!"

"And if they don't think it's wonderful?

"Well, we'll just have to keep acting like partners until they get it! You know, there's an irony here in this whole situation: I haven't felt respected. *I've* been fighting for recognition, but the same thing has been going on for years in this *department* that I just inherited. *It's* been tolerated and treated like an intruder. What a metaphor! The universe knew what it was doing when it gave me this job. We're both—my department and me—discovering a new purpose. We're both going to learn how to be partners in the next few months!"

Early indicators were that Sandy's new purpose was working. He started inviting former "enemies" to his staff meetings to coach his team on what they needed, and he offered to do the same with them. His boss welcomed the strategy with open arms and supported the partnership effort because he saw the potential for breakthrough.

As long as Sandy was operating out of his old purpose, to be tolerated, neither he nor his department could have broken out of the trap. By changing his purpose, he created a new possibility for himself, his co-workers and his company.

10

Janet

The Victim With a Black Belt

JANET HAD SPENT THE LAST THREE YEARS in Asia as a loyal spouse supporting her husband in his job as manager of an American venture. The problem was that she really didn't want to be there.

"I feel crushed and cramped all the time." She said, as we explored what was happening in her life. "There are so many people! I'd like a little space. You know they have ushers to cram you into the trains and subways. It's claustrophobic to me. I feel helpless almost all of the time."

"Helpless to do what?" I asked.

"Helpless to defend myself, for one thing. It's scary being pressed against so many people. And they won't back off. They just keep pressing."

"Sounds like a great experience you're having!"

"Oh, yeah! I don't want to be there, but Tom says it's only for a little while longer. But then he said that when we first arrived. 'Only one year, sweetheart, then they'll move me. I just have to get things started here." That was three years ago! I'm sick of this place. I just want to go home."

"You also said that you didn't particularly want to be

here, either, for this Intensive."

"Well, it looks to me like another one of those brainwashing sessions where the wife is sweet-talked into putting up with things just a little longer. I'm sick of being pushed around like that, too."

"It sounds like you're getting pushed around a lot in your life these days," I said.

"Yes. My life feels totally out of my control. I'm in a country where I don't want to be, with no friends I can relate to, nothing to do—and now here I am at this experience where I know I'm supposed to get enthusiastic about what's going on."

I asked her, "Without changing anything, how would you describe how you're sitting?"

Janet frowned. "Well, let's see… I'm slumped down in the sofa—it's hard to sit up in this thing, anyway—and I'm holding my hands in my lap. My feet are together kind of primly. I'm looking down at the floor a lot of the time." She chuckled. "Maybe I've been in Asia too long."

"What else do you notice about how you're holding yourself?"

"My voice is kind of quiet…"

"What about on the inside? What are you aware of in there?"

"Well, I'm a little scared. I'm frustrated. I feel pent up,

like I want to break out of a trap or something. I feel weak. It's all about being trapped where I am."

"Okay, Janet, it's important for you to know that I am under no instructions from Tom's boss or anyone else at the company to try to get you to be happy where you are. I would never accept that kind of secret agenda. I don't care where you live. What I care about is you finding a way to have more space and have a sense of freedom in your life. Do you believe me?"

"I don't know..."

"I think there is an opportunity here for you, even in the middle of your being stuck in Asia. Do you want to explore it?"

"I guess so. You said I'm in charge of what happens here. So I can stop you anytime I want, can't I?"

"Yep."

"Okay let's go. Where do we start?"

"What is it about the people that bugs you the most? That makes you want to get away from them?"

"They're so pushy...They are almost arrogant, always wanting to get their way, even if it's just to be first in line somewhere. There's this inevitability about them. They'll just keep pushing until they get what they want."

"How have you been coping?"

"I've learned the language, so I'm able to do the shopping, which is a real victory... Oh, I've taken Tae Kwon Do since I first arrived."

"That's a very powerful martial art, isn't it? What is that like for you?"

"It's been my salvation, really. I earned my Black Belt last month."

"A Black Belt! In three years! My Lord, Janet, that's incredible! Most people take ten years to get that far!"

"Well, I guess I was motivated. Plus I had all day to practice at the Dojo."

She was still sitting slumped down on the sofa with her hands in her lap and her eyes cast down. She looked weak and helpless. I thought, *How can this woman be a Black Belt in anything?*

I asked her about the Katas, the graceful movements designed to center the fighter and smooth out their skills. She said there was another name for them, but they were essentially the same things.

"What's your favorite?"

She named one and started to describe it verbally.

"Wait," I interrupted her. "Would you *show me* instead of telling me about it?"

"Sure."

She unfolded herself from the sofa, shoulders still hunched, and moved to the center of the room with her head down. Once there, she closed her eyes, pressed one fist into the other palm, took a deep, slow breath, stretched her body erect, threw her chest out and her shoulders back and opened her eyes slowly. She gazed out at the room with such concentration that her eyes looked like lasers. Standing there she was the epitome of relaxed concentration and power. Janet bowed slightly to some unseen figure (her sensei or teacher, I guessed). Then she began her movements, a series of blocks and strikes with her hands and feet, each one blending into the next, some so subtle I could hardly see them, some so fast her movements were a blur. Her feet flew out, she spun and pivoted, and her hands became a blinding whirl of hits and parries. Completely balanced, her eyes never faltered nor did she seem to lose contact with her center of focus.

Fascinated, I found myself thinking, in that state she could take on anyone I know (and I know some big, fast people). I was moved by her total concentration, the all-out power, the effortless grace, and the deep strength she emanated.

Wow! I thought. *Where has this woman been hiding?*

Gradually she slowed down and came to a stop, returning to her original position in the center of the room. She pressed her fist into her palm again, bowed slightly to the same unseen figure, took a deep breath, exhaled and... Right before my eyes her shoulders slumped, her head drooped, she settled back down into the sofa again, clasping her hands meekly, a lifeless, helpless, and weak figure.

"Wow!" I said, "That was really something. Thank you, Janet."

"Yes," she said so quietly that I could barely hear her. "It's very nice to do that."

"Very nice? Whew, it's very powerful!"

"I guess so", she murmured into her lap.

"Janet, that woman who was just here—where did she go?" I asked incredulously.

"What do you mean?" she looked at me curiously.

"That woman who did all those moves. Where did she go when you sat down?"

"I... I don't know."

"Are you aware of the difference in how you are when you're practicing Tae Kwon Do and how you are—now?"

"Well, no, not really... Now that you mention it, I do like being at the Dojo. I always feel a little better when I come out."

"How did you experience yourself *inside* just now when you were giving that demonstration?"

"Oh, wonderful!"

"How, specifically?"

"Calm, strong, capable, centered, safe...alive!"

"How would it feel to be in that state most of the time?"

"Oh, that's impossible!" She looked as if I'd said

something ludicrous.

"Why is that?"

"Well, that only happens during my Tae Kwon Do practices."

"What is the purpose of Tae Kwon Do?"

"It's to be in the presence of any kind of threat and be able to either defend yourself from harm or turn any attack into advantage."

"Sounds kind of like being in the middle of a culture which you experience as threatening you all the time!"

"Huh! I never thought of that! It is, kind of. In the Dojo I have taken attacks from many men much larger than myself, and—this is embarrassing—I've almost hurt a couple of them. How come I can face danger and force in the Dojo, even force aimed directly at me, and I can't in my everyday life? Isn't that strange?"

She was sitting on the edge of the sofa now, her eyes wide. We decided to differentiate the two identities that were a part of her. She named them The Victim and The Strong One. She described step-by-step how she shifted from one to the other. To do this, Janet had to slow down the process, then observe what she was doing with her breath, her muscles, her face, her eyes, all the little things that shifted as she made the transformation from one to the other. Soon she was standing in front of me as The Strong

One.

She reversed the process. Then I asked if she could do that in a restaurant or on the street or at home.

"I guess I could! I've just never done it consciously before."

She played with the roles, going back and forth. First: "Okay, stand by to meet—tah-dah—The Victim!"

She slumped, averted her eyes, and became The Victim.

"Now," I suggested, "what would The Strong One look like sitting there. How would she sit in that sofa? How would she interact with me?"

She shifted herself until she was seated fully upright, feet planted firmly on the floor. She looked directly at me, not in a challenging way, but with a strong, clear gaze. One hand was on the arm of the sofa, one in her lap. She appeared to be relaxed but ready for anything.

"How does that feel?" I asked.

"Great! This is great!"

As Janet looked at her current role as wife and supporter, she discovered that her feelings of helplessness stemmed not from people pressing in on her but on her husband's lack of understanding. He just didn't understand how much she wanted to be transferred. She felt helpless in her relationship with Tom.

"I have tried to get him to see what this place is doing to

me, and he just puts me off. I don't want to wreck his career, which he says would be 'off the rails' if he were to pull out early. So what am I to do?"

"Who's been talking with him, Janet? The Victim or The Strong One?"

"The Victim, for sure... I'm afraid when I talk with him. I know he won't listen before I start!"

She laughed. "Oh, no! It's all a matter of staying within yourself, not getting psyched out, just getting in the flow and doing what you can. The match takes care of itself!"

"Sounds like a great way to approach Tom, to me!"

"Yes, it does."

"Janet, if you lose a match, how do you feel? What kind of judgments do you lay on yourself?"

"Not many, actually. The key is how well I got into the flow, how I relaxed. If the other person wins, that's fine, as long as I relaxed and did my best."

The next morning Janet and Tom arrived in high spirits.

"What happened?" we asked.

"Well," Tom said, "we really got down to it last night. Janet told me in no uncertain terms that she didn't want to leave me, but that she might have to if she couldn't get me to listen to her. That got my attention. I'll tell you!"

Janet sat beside him, calm and attentive.

"Then she told me that she knew how important this job was to me but that it was killing her to be where we are. 'Which is more important, me or this job?' she asked me. I had to think about it! Usually I just wait her out, you know, let her get mad. Then she goes away and I breathe a sigh of relief. But this time she didn't leave. She stayed right there in my face and demanded an answer! For almost two hours!"

"My heart was beating hard," Janet said. "But I hung in there, breathing and staying clear about my love for Tom and for myself. It was scary but it was also exhilarating. I knew something new was going to happen."

"I'll say!" Tom said. "It was scary for me, too. I realized that I needed to respond to her. I've been taking her for granted for a long time. I see that now."

The outcome: Tom called his boss and told him he wanted a transfer. He was told that would be possible within ten months. Apparently that was enough for Janet.

"I can hold on for that long," she said, "knowing there's a light at the end of the tunnel. This has made it very clear: the issue wasn't really where I was living but my helplessness, which I can see was something I was doing to myself. At least I don't have to be helpless anymore about feeling helpless!"

Two years after he EDI, Janet reported she was in another country. "I'm teaching Tae Kwon Do," she told me, "and I'm a tour guide, leading a large group each month to different parts of this amazing country. I'm also fluent in the language! The best thing is, I'm enjoying my life."

11

Juliet

Learning to Dance Again

WHEN SHE WAS A GIRL, Juliet was a bundle of spontaneity. She had a natural playfulness that couldn't be contained. But that was a long time ago, long before she grew up and put away the childish things women learn they must put away in order to climb the executive ladder. Like Rachel, Juliet rose to the top of a Fortune 500 company. But whereas Rachel found herself a recipient of downsizing and re-engineering, Juliet found herself guiding the process at her company. It was a task for which she was eminently qualified.

Before her Intensive, it had never occurred to Juliet to reflect on how the playful girl became the no-nonsense woman. After all, hard work and hard trying were the norm in the corporate world, and Juliet had been handsomely rewarded for mastering the role of serious perfectionist. The executive she had become seemed the inevitable outcome of evolutionary forces.

But during a deeply reflective portion of her Intensive, Juliet wondered, "Where has that sunny little girl gone?" At one point her facilitator asked, "Where is that little girl inside of you, inside your body?"

Without hesitating, Juliet responded, "In my toes!" She

didn't know why she said it.

"In your toes?" asked the facilitator.

And then Juliet remembered. "In my toes," she said, recalling how much, as a very young girl, she loved to dance. Tap dance, ballet. Especially ballet. When Juliet danced, she danced really on the inside. It was an incredible feeling that Juliet's whole body, and especially her toes, had never forgotten. Just her mind had misplaced the memory.

"I loved the little fur pads we put in our pointe shoes to protect our toes," she said.

"Why did you stop?"

As clearly as if it had happened the day before instead of nearly half a century earlier, Juliet remembered a particular dance class. She wasn't yet a teenager. She was learning some new steps, struggling to get them right, and the instructor was scolding her, telling her sharply that she would never be a dancer... And that was when Juliet's perspective shifted. She had never looked at herself as a dancer from outside herself. She had only noticed the freedom and pleasure she felt inside her body as she spun and leaped and glided. Now, as though for the first time, she saw herself standing at the barre' with the other girls. As she studied herself in the mirror, she saw the mistake her instructor had seen. Her classmates continued to dance. Juliet just watched.

Only a few moments had passed, but for Juliet the dance

had vanished. In her place was Juliet, the serious observer, Juliet who wanted to be good, who would work hard and try hard and *make* herself succeed.

As soon as this recollection came to her, the corporate executive realized that not only had her body not truly danced in close to fifty years, neither had her spirit. The world of the little girl had collapsed into a narrow and intense mental space, which was still ruling her life. This realization came with a shattering awareness: "If I'm not *thinking*, I'm nothing." In the middle of her anguish, however, a profound thought from the Bible came to her, a thought which would allow her to release what had been imprisoned: "Be still and know that I am God."

During a break, Juliet went out and did something she figured she hadn't done in fifty years. "I got my fingernails painted."

She also decided to let herself dance again. This meant literally dancing, by herself, as a form of exercise. She loved it and found it effortless, even after all these years. But she also wanted to express herself more at work. That meant, "letting myself be more free in my contribution"—instead of out of consideration for others' judgment of her.

"It suddenly occurred to me that my life is not about thinking hard and trying hard. It's about being—and getting in touch with—the spirit that is me."

Juliet the dancer had reappeared.

Recently, she was scheduled to give a presentation at corporate headquarters. Before, she might have labored over her preparation endlessly, agonizing over getting every last detail just right. But this time, just two hours before the presentation, she jotted an outline that would allow for the most spontaneous flow.

Moreover, the day before, she had received an e-mail notice from her boss, Elizabeth, alerting Juliet that she would be attending the presentation.

"I think before the Intensive I would have been very worried about, 'What is Elizabeth going to think?' Wanting to impress her, wanting to live up to her standards. Now that didn't matter at all. I was just looking forward to Elizabeth's company and to having her participate. I gave her my outline and told her to feel free to jump in at any time. She did, and we had a wonderful interactive presentation. I couldn't believe how relaxed I felt and the positive feedback I got. It wasn't perfect, It was alive—and real.

12

George

Working for Love, Not Thanks

GEORGE'S CAREER WITH THE COMPANY was a mixed blessing for him. He had done an outstanding job at his specialty, strategic planning, was promoted to vice president, and now had the ear and respect of his boss. Down deep George was a change agent committed to doing whatever he could to help other employees and the company be the best they could be.

Over the years he had provided a constant source of ideas about how to improve things. Recently he had shifted from being content with slow, incremental change to seeking breakthrough, fundamental re-thinking of the company's business.

Anytime you take a stand for creating fundamental change, you run the risk of making some people mad, but in George's case he had really dug a hole for himself.

When he started his campaign in his division, he had done so because the human resources (HR) vice president wasn't interested. Such change efforts would normally originate with the HR division. So when George began to sense the need for something more proactive, he gradually stepped into this void. The HR guy was relieved that he didn't have to get into the messy process of change; George was excited to be able to expand his focus. When a new VP for the HR function came aboard, he told George, "Keep HR informed and in the decision-making loop, and you can keep initiating change projects for now."

The main problem for George was this: when he tried to sell his colleagues on his concepts, he made them mad. There was something about the way he went about it. Co-workers called George arrogant and a know-it-all. "What makes him think he's got all the answers?" one of them asked me. "He acts as if what we're doing is all *wrong* and he's all *right*."

In his Intensive, George confessed, "I've about had it with these people!"

"What's the problem?"

"They just don't get it..."

"Don't get what?"

"What I've been trying to show them; that they have to become more attuned to the need for ongoing fundamental change. They seem to think they can keep doing things the same old way. Hell, I don't know all the answers, but I do know we've got to try to find them!"

"So, what's the problem?"

"I'm getting pissed off. They sit in the meetings and nod their heads when I'm talking, but after the meeting they just bad-mouth my ideas."

"That's all about *them*. What happens to *you* in all this?" I asked.

"You know what really bugs me? It's their lack of acknowledgment. They never tell me that I'm doing anything helpful. They never say, 'Keep up the good work, George.' All I get from them is resistance and behind-the-back ambushes."

"If you had to label them in one word, what would you call them?"

"Ungrateful. They're ungrateful. They can't see or appreciate the good things I've done for them. They don't appreciate the value I bring to our work. I'm helping them and they're mad at me! Well ____ them!"

"You're expecting at least a little gratitude for all you're doing for them."

"Yeah... Is that too much to ask?"

I played a hunch and asked George if he ever had an experience of helping people and not caring if they were grateful to him.

"Yes, I have," he answered slowly. His face and voice softened. "Every summer my wife and I serve as volunteer staff at a camp for mentally and physically disadvantaged adults. Many of them can't...you know, they can't..." His voice broke a little. "They can't do the simplest things. Tie their shoes. Wipe themselves. Put their clothes on. Stuff like that. Sometimes I don't even *do* anything; I just sit or stand beside them."

Tears flowed down his cheeks as he visualized these scenes. "They often don't even know or care that I'm there. Sometimes they do. Sometimes one of them will just walk up and hug me, stroke my arm, talk to me about their day, smile and then walk off. And it's okay. I'm not there to get their appreciation. It's not about them really; it's about me. It *is* about them in that I'm there for them, but I don't have any agenda or expectation for them. I'm just serving because it's in me to serve them. It's love, that's all, just love." He recalled the feeling he'd had when he was at camp. "I feel alive! Good inside... Peaceful... Happy... Satisfied..."

"Picture doing something with one of the campers... Got something? Okay, tell me what's happening as if it's going on right now."

"I'm walking up to this young man and he's trying to tie his shoes—with great difficulty. I'm asking him if he wants any help. He nods. I bend over..."

"What's going on in your mind right now?" I interjected. "What are you thinking as you start to help him?"

"I'm thinking, 'Boy, I'm glad I can be here doing this!'"

"Any thoughts like, 'He's sure going to appreciate me when I'm done,' or 'He's got to like this!'?"

"Nope... Nothing like that... I'm just feeling happy to be here doing what I'm doing. It's almost as if I'm doing it for myself in some way, not to get him to give me something. Just *doing it* will be its own reward..."

"Now picture you're getting ready to do something at work, like initiating a change project. What goes through your mind?"

He laughed as he spoke. "I'll bust my butt on this thing and they'll either resist me every step of the way or pretend to go along but sabotage it behind the scenes and make jokes about, 'There goes George again, trying to save the world.' I'm ticked off before I even begin, and not very hopeful about the success of the project, either."

"What would happen if you acted with them like you do at summer camp?"

George was silent for a few moments. "If I could pull that off, it'd be great... I would still do what I'm doing now, but it wouldn't be connected to my colleagues' reactions at all."

George told me recently that he hasn't been angry at people at work in a long time. He's been doing his work as usual, and co-workers are still responding as usual. But suffering over a lack of appreciation isn't an issue for him anymore. "I'm finding so much joy in doing what I'm doing... It's not as if I don't still want to be acknowledged, but just making a difference--one that I can acknowledge--is getting to be enough for me."

He still has what we call "attacks," where he gets hooked

for a moment, but it passes quickly.

One of the most significant developments is that the corporate group, which for three years had resisted change projects he recommended, came to him with what seemed like a new idea. "They actually asked me to do a project I've been blunting my pick on since 1990. I can't believe it! Wonder if it has anything to do with my not needing to change them anymore...?"

Moreover, he says, "I'm having fun again. I know my work is making a difference, even when nobody else sees the value in it."

13

Hank

From Looking Good to Being Real

WE SPENT MOST OF HANK'S FIRST DAY looking at what he wanted to achieve. "I need to develop my ability to bring out the best in those who aren't cutting it," he told me. It seemed he was comfortable with star performers but had difficulty supervising below-average employees.

On the second day, we cut to the core. "The feedback I get is puzzling to me." Hank began. "I've heard that I'm aloof and stuck up. One boss told me I was arrogant. That sure doesn't jibe with what's going on inside."

Inside his own head, Hank definitely did not feel better than anybody else. He intensely wanted to please people by doing his job well. He sometimes felt scared that he wasn't measuring up. So how was it people got the impression he was self-important?

I asked if he was aware of the way that he speaks, the way he formed sentences.

"What do you mean? Am I using bad grammar or something like that?"

"Oh, no, just the opposite. Don't change anything, but for the next few minutes just listen to yourself speak and see what you notice."

He said he didn't notice anything unusual. "I didn't make any mistakes in my diction at all."

"Is that an issue? Making mistakes in diction? Because what I notice is your being what I would call *cautious* in your speaking. You seem to choose your words carefully, as if you were writing a paper for an English class or giving a speech before Congress or something. You rarely use any slang or figures of speech, and you speak in complete sentences. It's not spontaneous talking, but self-conscious. Does that ring any bells?"

"Well, I don't want to use poor grammar . . ."

"What would happen," I asked, "if you used poor grammar?" He looked at me curiously.

"Well, people would think I was stupid or came from the wrong side of the tracks or something like that."

"Now where does that come from? Are you from the wrong side of the tracks?"

Long pause. He looked out the window, his attention far away. When he began to speak, his words were slow, quiet, and even more thoughtful than before.

"I *was* born on the wrong side of town, in a sense. My mother and father were good people, but my father had a laborer's job. I guess you could say we were poor. We had a small a house—almost a shack, really. That often embarrassed me.

"Then my father got a better job, and I think we came into some small inheritance. My parents offered me the chance to go to a private prep school nearby. Not my brother, just me. It was as if they wanted me to break out on behalf of all of them." He began to weep. "They did that for me . . . I felt I *had* to make good . . . For them . . ."

At the new prep school the other kids made fun of Hank— the way he dressed, the way he talked, they laughed at everything about him. At first he was crushed, feeling he didn't belong. Then he got mad. He said to himself, "They're not going to get me! I'm going to rise above this. I'm going to be as good as they are, or even better!"

From then on, Hank was a manager. Every time he walked into a room, he managed an internal dialogue. *Okay, pal, don't mess up. Don't give them a single thing to fault you on. Dress better than they do, speak better than they do, do everything correctly. No mistakes. No slips. No loss of concentration. If you eliminate every cause for criticism, they can't hurt you.* That's what he thought. And it worked.

He was elected class president and made the honor roll. When he graduated and went to work with a Fortune 100 company he knew he had finally made it!

Hank had been on the fast track ever since. He was in charge of the fastest-growing division in the company and was in line for the presidency.

"I've even surprised myself," he told me. "My wife seems to be the only one who isn't surprised!"

"Is this strategy, developed in prep school, still successful for you?" I asked.

"Now that you mention it, I can see that I am always making sure that I don't make a mistake, even about little things, like the way I dress. I think before I speak. I want to put people at ease around me. I guess I'm keeping myself under control so I won't give anyone anything they could fault me for. That's it. I'm being careful not to give people a reason for judging me or ridiculing me."

"So your strategy is working. Are there any costs involved?"

"Well, it sounds like one cost is that I come across as arrogant. That's amazing to me, but I'm beginning to see how they could get that idea . . . It may be that in my mind I have to be *better* than everyone else *just to have a right to be around.*"

"Another thing is that I feel like I have to be 'on' all the time. I can't let down, even for a second, or else I might make a slip and say or do something that's not correct. It's exhausting actually."

His mind was now fully engaged. Hank noticed he was sick and tired of needing to appear perfect all the time.

"How badly do you want to change all this, Hank? It seems to be working for you. Is it worth letting go of?"

"I'm ready, but it's scary to think about who I'd be if I stop trying to be perfect! I mean, would I turn into some kind of monster or something? Maybe it's a good thing that I hold myself in all the time."

"What are you afraid might happen if you let go?"

"I don't know . . . Something bad, though . . ."

I suggested he confront his own worst fear. In this case it was that he might appear stupid in front of his boss, Ben. A good man. Hank proceeded to carry on an imaginary conversation with Ben, telling him what had been happening.

"Ben, I have a confession to make. I have been tiptoeing around you—actually, around everybody—for a long time, trying to act in such an appropriate way that I would never give you cause to criticize me. I wanted to appear *perfect* to you and to everybody else."

"Now, move over and sit in Ben's chair and respond to 'Hank' . . ." He shifted to Ben's chair and looked back to where he had been sitting.

"Hank, you have always been appropriate, that's not a problem. The problem is that you come across like a know-it-all. You're so well rehearsed that no one can relate to you! You seem phony. I don't know what's really going on with you. Who's behind the perfect facade, Hank?"

He switched chairs again.

"Ben, it's lonely back here . . . and a little scary. I think 'What if he finds out that I don't have the answer?' or 'What if I screw up?' It's hard being on stage all the time."

Ben spoke again.

"Hank, just relax. I know you don't have it all together all the time. That's okay with me. Welcome to the human race! I've found myself wishing you would fail or something—not a big thing, mind you—just so you could discover what that's like. Here's the toughest thing I have to say to you: If you keep up this way, it's going to affect your career."

He stared hard at "Hank" as he went on.

"Your perfection is leading you to possible failure. Trying so hard to look good is making you look bad. We need you to lighten up."

The mask dropped and the real Hank was filled with a deep sadness.

"John, I don't know how to stop trying to be perfect."

"If you didn't want to be perfect all the time, what would you want to be?"

"I don't want to *have* to be perfect all the time and I don't want to be imperfect, either."

"Are you perfect, or are you someone trying to be

perfect?"

"Oh, I'm clearly someone trying to be perfect!"

"So, who is it that's trying to be perfect? Who's in there making this valiant effort to be so appropriate?"

When Hank thought about who was behind the front, who was the one working so hard to look perfect, speaking so carefully, dressing so meticulously, he came back around to a very simple idea. If he put aside all the striving, "I guess I'd just be *me* . . . Whoever *that* is . . ."

All at once he smiled and visibly relaxed.

"Oh, man! I don't know what's going on, but I feel great! It's as if a big weight has been lifted off my shoulders. Right now I don't really care whether you see me as appropriate or not."

Of course, this conversation has been compressed for the purpose of this book. But over the course of the Intensive, Hank had a chance to practice a new, unrehearsed way of being. He found it was actually possible to speak without first mulling over his diction. He didn't have to pay attention to what his hands were doing. In fact, when he realized he didn't have to consciously manipulate the direction and expression of his eyes, he said, "Holy cow, I had no idea I was doing *that* all the time! No wonder I get so tired!" That's a lot to keep track of, and it doesn't seem to be working anyway! What a joke . . .What a relief!"

His new assignment was not to worry about changing

anything about himself. He wasn't supposed to even try to stop himself from thinking about being appropriate. That would be more of the same. Then he'd have something *new* to be on the lookout for—trying to be appropriate! He could make himself feel wrong for that and be back in the same trap.

Worrying about being appropriate wasn't going to change overnight. Like the skin on a snake, when the new skin is ready underneath, the old skin just sloughs off naturally. The beginning for Hank was to simply observe his inner conversation and practice choosing what to do next.

Since that conversation, Hank has had many opportunities to test his new strategy, to just "be myself and let the chips fall where they may." He turned down a chance to go back to the home office for a promotion because he said, "It sounded like more of the same to me," and he wanted something different.

"Before, I would have taken that promotion without even a thought. It would have been my just reward for all the hard work. But this time I asked myself what I really wanted. And the answer was to let my family stay where we are and let the kids finish school."

His decision impressed Ben, who commented to me about it afterward. "We've got big plans for Hank. He'll be better off staying where he is for awhile, anyway."

The numerical results in this case were also positive. His division surpassed all predictions several years in a row. This might have happened anyway, but Hank believes that his new awareness, his new sense of who he really is, down deep, and his willingness to be whoever that is, has been a significant factor in his and his divisions success. He says he can see things clearer now that he's not planning how to impress people all the time, and that his decisions, especially concerning personnel, are much more on target.

His relationships with his peers and subordinates also shifted dramatically, according to both his and their accounts. His direct reports say things like, "I don't know what happened out there, in Spokane, but Hank is sure better to work with. He doesn't seem so stuck on himself, so cock-sure all the time. It's like he's become a human being!"

Four years after his Intensive, Hank recalled a vivid impression of his first day in Spokane. "The other facilitator said to me, 'It looks like staying in control is a big thing with you.' I was stunned at how she pegged it so fast. 'How can you tell?' I asked her. And she said, 'I notice that you finish the ends of your sentences and words very carefully, and when you breathe, your chest doesn't move at all.'

"The part about my chest not moving was also a surprise and has turned out to be important. I catch myself holding my breath from time to time when things are tense. So I just relax, take a long, slow breath and consciously open my chest. It helps me open my heart to whatever's happening, too."

He finished by saying that spiritual integrity has become a daily consideration. "I used to be pretty down on religion. It wasn't rational. But I've found a faith now that fits for me and has become an important part of my life. Developing myself intellectually, physically, and spiritually is now more important to me than getting to be corporate president."

Conclusion

Don't Shoot the Phantom

ABOUT TWO HUNDRED PEOPLE have been through the Executive Development Intensive. In a way, they were like solo performers in a one-character play put on in a tiny theater with no audience but themselves. Each of the performers experienced a drama that was uniquely their own.

But the themes of each of these dramas were all pretty much the same. And the themes would be the same—I feel safe in saying this—for any of ten thousand people you might recruit off the street at random anywhere. This is because it's a timeless theme. It's about discovering a distinction between who we *think* we are and—well, let's just say someone else. Finding out about this distinction is usually very interesting. Sometimes it's life changing.

From the time we were born, each of us went into training to *be somebody*. Who we trained to be depends on the circumstances we were born into and the sense we make of those circumstances. Psychologists estimate that by the end of early childhood the average person has had *twenty-five thousand hours* of pure, unadulterated programming from parents or whoever is doing the child rearing. Obviously, plenty of the early messages we receive were never even consciously given, were never anything more than the reflexive behavior of caregivers stumbling alongtrying to make their own way in the world. ("We're all just trying to make it to the post office," my Pop used to tell me.) But conscious or otherwise, we sponge up these early messages.

I don't think it would be too farfetched to say that instead of being the home of five billion people, the Earth has become the home of five billion phantoms. The phantoms aren't doing a very good job of running the place. It's not their fault. They aren't qualified for the job.

But I don't think we should shoot our phantoms, or fire them, or try to run them out of town or anything like that. What they need is love and understanding. They're not trying to hurt anybody; they're doing their best to help. There is something we like to tell people. "Our task is not to transform you," we say. "Our task is to love you. The love itself will transform you."

Fight the phantom and he or she will resist you. Phantoms are formidable adversaries, martial artists of the psyche. Fortunately, behind the phantom is another self, our *real* self, and our true spirit. This is what we need to get reacquainted with.

I certainly don't want to suggest there's only one way this reunion can take place. Far from it. People have life-changing encounters with their inner selves all the time. Trauma, therapy, unconditional love, a spontaneous spiritual experience triggered by anything or nothing at all—all can be a catalyst. There are probably an infinite number of ways to meet up with yourself again.

Even without those prompts, however, there are some first steps a person can take to awaken and nurture the spirit. The following list was put together in collaboration with a good friend and colleague of mine, Mark Kelso. It is a simple recipe with five ingredients.

1. **Solitude:** Find a way to spend ten to fifteen minutes a day alone with yourself. Take a walk, sit with a cup of tea, or look out the window. Do anything you enjoy, anything that, for you, is a reward in itself.

2. **Exercise:** Do fifteen to twenty minutes of enjoyable, vigorous, fresh air exercise every day.

3. **Nutrition:** Eat consciously and moderately. Learn to listen to what your body wants.

4. **Stewardship:** Become a conscious steward of what has been given to you: your body, your spouse and children, your house, friends, pets, garden, car, money—even your staff, if you are a manager. Just ask, "What have I been given to manage in my life?"

5. **Service:** Each week, make a significant contribution to the larger family of the world—time, money, or both--to others outside your immediate family. It needs to be significant to you, and done without regard for recognition from others.

What this recipe will get you is some attention from yourself. Most of us don't get much of this, certainly not enough to allow us to discern that still, small voice that often has some pretty good advice if we'll just be *quiet* for half a minute.

And it will get you some air, some oxygen. If you are not now exercising daily, you need more air than you are getting; your spirit needs more, because your spirit is in your muscles and your synapses and every part of you. Isn't it interesting that the word "spirit" has the same root as "in-spire" and "ex-pire", which has to do with *breathing*. (Competitive sports don't usually qualify here because the phantom is usually engaged.) Maybe you shouldn't think of it as exercise, but think of it as mindful movement. Become a connoisseur of oxygen. Learn to breathe. The breath has been called "the leash of the ego."

As for nutrition, it's not only what you eat that matters but *why* you eat. What does the food represent to you? Unbalanced eating is fueled by something besides hunger—love, security, or whatever, which the psyche, the phantom, is craving. You can never eat enough to satisfy the phantom. The body knows better, so learn to notice what the body wants.

Conscious stewardship, respecting your personal realm of influence, will help to bring you in touch with yourself.

Service to others will bring you back into community, which is something the spirit needs and yearns for. You are connected to the entire universe, and the spirit knows this. The phantom doesn't. The spirit seeks communion and wholeness, which is everyone's birthright.

The cumulative impact of this simple recipe is to create a tiny bit of separation between you and your phantom self. The five steps aren't destinations in themselves. But if you start doing these things, whatever else you need to do will come to you.

To all of the above a general caveat applies. Don't do it— don't do *any* of it—because you should. That will be self-defeating. Do it for the inherent rewards. Only when your external success is a by-product of your inner personal growth will that success fulfill you. Or, to paraphrase Jesus, "Seek first the kingdom within, and then all the other things you need will be given to you."

Work and the human spirit. I can imagine two basic questions, one asked by individuals, one asked by companies.

To individuals who would ask, "Why should I nurture my spirit?" I can only answer, "I don't know. I can't presume to know for anyone else." It's an extremely personal matter. If you already feel sustained in your spirit, or if for whatever reason it is not an issue for you, great! If it is, then I hope something in this book has been useful to you.

I think it's a different matter with regard to companies,

however. As I said at the outset, I think companies have gotten about as far as they can by pursuing external results alone. The instrument panel of too many companies monitor only the outer world of goals, the bottom line, not the inner conditions which determine if the goals can be reached. It's a little like running a car without ever looking at your oil pressure or water temperature.

To illustrate: Companies are spending an arm and a leg these days on team training and participative management. This is because modern forces of the marketplace are making the ability to collaborate and partner with others prerequisites for success and even survival. The other day, George, whose story is told in Chapter 12, told me something interesting. He said it's pretty hard to collaborate with co-workers if you're not in touch with yourself, because otherwise you're probably so busy trying to beat everyone out that you don't really have time to collaborate.

The phantom is not a team player. The phantom strives to be an island of competitive competence.

Are the implications really all that revolutionary? In a way, I suppose they are: as we become more skilled at managing our inner worlds, frantic efforts at manipulating the outer world will fail and the world we see around us will be very different. But in another sense, the hunch on which this book is based isn't radical at all. (The hunch is that the quality of work we do cannot be separated from the quality of self we manage to create.)

A Canadian colleague, Art McNeil, calls the kind of self-reflection recorded in this book, "a lifetime commitment to renew the *person* behind the *position*." There are companies who have been acting on this understanding for a long time. One manager of a hotel, which is world-famous for its customer service, explained: "We hire people very carefully. We can teach people what to *do*. We can't teach them what to *be*."

ACKNOWLEDGMENTS

LARRY SHOOK—for seeing so clearly and for turning concept into reality.

JUDY LADDON—for the reminder of the power of parable—insisting that the "meat" of this book was in the stories—and for fearless editing.

"CARL" —for making the simple request that led me to explore solo body/mind/spirit executive development.

"HANS" —for being the first and jumping in with both feet.

PIETER TER HAAR—for launching his ARK and showing the way.

BILL MCKENDREE—for helping us turn an *ad hoc* executive intensive experience into a real program with a plan and a future.

CAROL RADY—for championing the work so relentlessly.

BOB HESLIN—for continuing to believe that this kind of digging is worthwhile.

DOUG HENCK—for never-ending support and for insisting that spouses' participation be mandatory.

JEANANNE OLIPHANT—for creating new ways of bringing this approach to work.

EARL GOODE—for launching his company-wide leadership development effort by sending his senior management teams to the EDI.

NANCY FRAUHIGER & GREGG DABICCI-- for suggesting it.

DIXON DE LEÑA—for the coaching about the power of commitment and the process of transformation and for the invitation to change my own Formula for Success.

ALISON RUBIN—for holding it all together in the early years and ensuring that the Body was never left out.

THE EDI GRADUATES—for having the courage to explore inner space.

DIXON, ALISON, BARBARA & DAN BAUMGARTEN, DAYA SCHERER, MENKA MACLEOD, NICK WOLFSON, TED BUFFINGTON & CHANDRA SMITH—pioneer core facilitators, whose tough love has touched so many human spirits.

GURUDEV—for the many conversations at the crack of dawn.

JONATHAN FOUST, CAROLYN DELUOMO, RICHARD MICHAELS, HAROLD KARPFEN, PEGGY SCHELDAHL, DOUG SCHON, BEV OWENS, JOEL FELDMAN, MICHAEL LEE, AND THE REST OF THE KRIPALU TEAM—for putting the path into action.

NANCE GUILMARTIN—for being the catalyst and for taking it to the world.

MELISSA HAYDEN—for maintaining calm in the storm.

GREGORY DIX—for believing early on.

RICK HOSMER, BRIAN GAGE AND DARIN KLUNDT—for the heart invested in cover design.

RADM LYLE BULL (RET.), CHIEF BRIAN O'KELLEY, & LT. DAVE ROBINSON—for helping keep the Phantom story accurate thirty years after the fact.

JIM HESLEP, KATHLEEN HANCOCK, JEANETTE HENNA, HOMER BAST, STANLEY KRIPPNER, FRANK VEST AND GEORGE ANDERSON—for seeing someone who couldn't yet see himself.

J.J.—for showing what faith-in-action could look like.

SISTER RUTH—for teaching me about selfless service and unconditional love.

POP—for the enjoyment of words and ideas, and the ability to share the common cup of humanity.

BOONE—for never giving up and for teaching us how to move on when it's over.

JAY, DAVID, ASA, AND EMMA—for creating so many opportunities to practice as a father

CATH—for living it and for holding my feet to the fire of marriage.

About the Authors

John Scherer is one of America's most innovative applied behavioral scientists and management consultants. He is founder of the Executive Development Intensive and author of *The Breakthrough Video Series*. An honors graduate of Roanoke College and Lutheran Theological Southern Seminary, John co-founded one of the nation's first graduate programs in the field. His corporate clients have included GTE, AEtna, the GAO, Ace Hardware, Marriott, Polaroid, the U.S. Army, and many others. Before beginning his consulting work, he was an officer on a destroyer in the Navy and Lutheran Chaplain at Cornell University. He is married to Catharine Scherer and has four children; Jay, David, Asa, and Emma.

In past years, writer Larry Shook has been editor of *Washington Magazine, Seattle Weekly, San Diego Magazine,* co-publisher and editor of *Spokane Magazine,* and has written for such publications as *The New York Times, Washington Post* and *People Magazine.* He has collaborated with John Scherer on many projects. Author of *The Puppy Report*, he lives in Spokane with his wife Judy, children Ben and Katie, and dogs, Millie and Durango.

Author's Note

The EXECUTIVE DEVELOPMENT INTENSIVE (EDI) has been evolving ever since "Hans" (see Chapter 1) made his life-changing trip to Spokane in 1987. Virtually every participant since then, has expressed a desire for a way to make such an experience available for their middle managers. As a result, in 1994 we created a group version of the program, called the Leadership Development Intensive (LDI). The curriculum is an exact replica of the EDI (except for the daily massage!), conducted with 16-20 men and women from various organizations. Post-LDI research indicates that graduates enjoy the same kind of life-changing experiences created in the solo program.

Several Organizations in the U.S. and Canada, have decided to make the LDI a part of their "fast-tracker" program. They want to make sure their high potential managers are challenged to address the human factor as they move into higher leadership positions.

What We Do:

Executive Leadership Development

Integrated Merger Processes

Culture Change Projects

Peak Performance Consulting

Conflict Resolution

High Performance Team Building

Keynote Presentations

For Further information, products, or services please contact:

John Scherer & Associates

421 W. Riverside Suite1000

Spokane, WA 99201

Toll-Free 1-800-727-9115

Phone (509) 838-8167

Fax (509) 623-2511

info@jsassociates.com

www.jsassociates.com